CHRISTIAN ENCOUNTERS SERIES

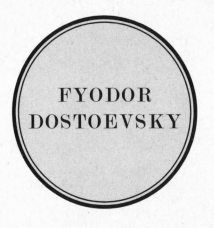

FYODOR DOSTOEVSKY

CHRISTIAN ENCOUNTERS SERIES

FYODOR DOSTOEVSKY

PETER LEITHART

THOMAS NELSON
Since 1798

NASHVILLE   DALLAS   MEXICO CITY   RIO DE JANEIRO

Published in Nashville, Tennessee, by Thomas Nelson. Thomas Nelson is a
registered trademark of Thomas Nelson, Inc.

Thomas Nelson, Inc., titles may be purchased in bulk for educational, business,
fund-raising, or sales promotional use. For information, please e-mail
SpecialMarkets@ThomasNelson.com.

Library of Congress Cataloging-in-Publication Data

Leithart, Peter J.
  Fyodor Dostoevsky / Peter Leithart.
    p. cm. — (Christian encounters)
  ISBN 978-1-59555-034-7
  1. Dostoevsky, Fyodor, 1821–1881. I. Title.
PG3328.L38 2011
891.73'3--dc22
  [B]   2011007476

Printed in the United States of America

11 12 13 14 15 16 HCI 6 5 4 3 2 1

To Vivian Joyce Leithart

"Lay waste with fire the heart of man."

CONTENTS

AUTHOR'S NOTE

Conversations in *Fyodor Dostoevsky*, unless specifically cited from another work, were created by the author as a literary device and are to be read as fictionalized accounts of his life. As will be evident, the story is told in two time frames. Conversations between Dostoevsky and Apollon Maikov are set in 1888, on the eve of Dostoevsky's trip to Moscow for the Pushkin festival, but the conversations are interspersed with flashbacks to key events in Dostoevsky's life. Also, variations of Russian names are common throughout the book.

1

FAINTING SOUL

Fyodor Mikhailovich Dostoevsky slid his straight-backed, heavy wooden chair away from the table, swiveled sideways, and crossed his legs. He let out a satisfied sigh. Dinner was finished, and his wife Anna, and daughter Lyubov were clearing things away. His son Fedya was outside exploring the rocky banks of the river in the light of the setting sun. Dostoevsky was left at the table with his vodka and poet and friend Apollon Maikov.

"Thank you, Anna," Maikov said. Dostoevsky abstract-edly nodded his assent.

Through the open window, they could hear the gentle murmur of the Pererititsa as it lazied past. A night of polishing and editing lay ahead of him, but Fyodor was not ready to move to his desk. He wanted to continue the argument that had begun at dinner, an argument about Russia. It was good preparation for the coming week, most excellent preparation.

"I am convinced," he told Maikov, "that Russia has been

preserved for just this time. I tell you there is something in the Russian soul, something good."

"Turgenev has written . . ." Maikov began.

"Turgenev! Turgenev! Don't quote Turgenev. You know he's become almost my personal enemy." Fyodor raised his voice. "What does he know of the Russian people? He has no sympathy with them. How can he? His tutors were French and Germans! He's been viewing us through a telescope for years, from his porch in Baden."

"Come, come, Fyodor! That is unfair." Maikov removed his glasses and wiped them on his shirt front.

"No. I told him the same to his face. It is true, absolutely true. He has forgotten one of his fatherlands."

Maikov looked puzzled.

"We Russians have two fatherlands, Russia and Europe."

"You will offend both Turgenev and the Slavophiles with words like that."

Dostoevsky scoffed. "It is the simplest truth. We have two fathers—Vladimir is the Russian father, our Orthodox father, but then Peter is our second father, who gave us a second birth, our European father. We have two fathers and two fatherlands, and that is what makes Russia unique among all nations. It makes us a universal people."

"With two fathers, we are more likely monstrous."

Dostoevsky smiled, but he was too deep into the argument to let it diffuse. "This is what everyone misses, everyone. Both the devils and the old romantics, like Turgenev, miss it on one side, chasing every Western ghost. And the Slavophiles miss it on the other side. Unless we see that we have two fathers, we will never be the Russia we're destined to be. There will always be the literary men on the one side, reading their Balzac and their Hugo and their Dickens and Marx and Engels, and the peasants on the other reading next to nothing at all, listening to folk tales and hiding from devils."

"But Tolstoy, of course. Tolstoy grasps the Russian character. He knows the heart of the Russian peasant."

"No! He knows nothing of them, despite his peasant airs and his beard and his boots. He's not a novelist or poet, not really. He's an historian, and he has no contact with the heart of Russia. Tolstoy is a count; Turgenev's family has wealth and social status. Even Gogol was the son of a gentry father and a mother who descended from Polish nobility. I am the son of a medical doctor, hardly a distinguished profession. Of course, far, far back my family is descended from the Lithuanian nobility, but we have declined far from that. Many of my ancestors served as priests in the Uniat church. Did you know that?"

Maikov nodded. "Your father did register you and your brother in the directory."

"Yes, but that was hard-won. He gained his noble status because of distinguished medical service. He wasn't born to it, nor was I. I didn't have any tutors, and my first adult acquaintances were my father's poor, pathetic patients at the hospital. I'd visit with them while they sat in the garden and listen to their stories."

Maikov knew Fyodor was in one of his aggressive moods, raging like Achilles. He took a sip of vodka and waited for him to continue. Dostoevsky poured water and took a drink. "Anna's veal was delicious, but it made me so thirsty." Dostoevsky coughed, setting off a deep rattle in his chest.

"Pushkin. Pushkin was different," he continued. "He was as highborn as any of them, and he knew the West and all their poets. But he knew the Russian heart and spoke directly to the Russian people." Fyodor stood, raised a hand, and adopted a pose.

> "With fainting soul athirst for Grace,
> I wandered in a desert place,
> And at the crossing of the ways
> I saw a sixfold Seraph blaze;
> He touched mine eyes with fingers light
> As sleep that cometh in the night."[1]

"Yes, Pushkin was a prophet. He had his muse."

"Russia was his muse. Russia was his lady, the muse of all his desires. No one in Russia can see that. But that poem is my confession. I have seen that seraph and felt his burning touch. I know the Russian people, know them like no other writer today."

Fyodor rolled a cigarette, lit it, and sucked in the calming smoke. As smoke curled around his moustache, he asked, "Have I ever told you about Marey the peasant?"

≈

"Darovoe! We're going to Darovoe!"

Mikhail, Fyodor, and Andrey all sighed and stared out the

window of the carriage as it clattered past the last houses of Moscow. Behind them lay the cramped rooms and low ceilings of the Dostoevsky home. Behind them was Dr. Dostoevsky, busy with his patients at the Mariinsky Hospital for the Poor. Dr. Dostoevsky was as stiff as his collar, with his military, monotonous, demanding regimen—up at six, lessons until lunch when they would have to stand erect to endure an exacting review from Father, lessons all afternoon, dinner at nine, prayers before the icons, bed, then up at six and the whole joyless round again and again. Behind this regimen were all the suppressed tensions that simmered beneath the surface of Dostoevsky propriety. Behind them were Father's irritable rages, his tirades at the slightest error in Latin or arithmetic. He never hit them, but his insults were painful. "Sluggards and fools," he would roar, and Fyodor's heart would whirl in confusion—eager to please, resentful, rebellious, then guilty for his resentfulness and bitterness, all at once. Sometimes he wanted to disappear, or die.

In good weather, Dr. Dostoevsky took his children for a walk in the evening, but even then Father frowned sternly if they began to run or wrestle or behave in any manner unbefitting to respectability and family honor. Home in Moscow, Fyodor stayed indoors most of the time, and he never ventured out without his father.[2]

But now they were going to Darovoe, the Dostoevsky country estate. There a boy could stretch his legs, run, roam, explore. There he could be free. No wonder the boys greeted every trek to Darovoe with ecstatic excitement.[3]

Life in Moscow was not without its joys, Fyodor thought as

he listened to the bells jingling on the horses' harness. Often it was happy. Mother made it happy. Mother was with them in the carriage to Darovoe.

With her natural gaiety, kindness, and compassion, Marya Fyodorovna Dostoevsky made up for what her strict, anxious husband lacked.[4] She, too, was eager to visit Darovoe. Since her husband had bought the property the previous year, in 1831, she had found it a place where she could be useful. She was heartbroken at the living conditions of the peasants on the estate, and she did all she could—too much, her husband scolded—to ease their lot. She provided seed for the peasants to plant and then dug a canal to make it easier for the peasants to get water. She enlisted her sons in the same ministry, sending Fyodor to fetch water for a woman who had just had a baby or to help gather firewood for an injured peasant.

Fyodor was looking thoughtfully across the carriage at his mother. "Tell us again how you and Father met," he said.

Mother smiled and reached over to smooth her son's gingery hair. "It's not much of a story, Fyodor. Our families arranged it all ahead of time. The first time we met was the day our families decided to betroth us."

"You weren't in love when you married, then?" Mikhail asked.

"We barely knew each other."

"But you love him now, don't you?" Andrey butted in.

Marya blushed. Mikhail, her husband, was a difficult man, too hard on the children, too stingy with his servants. But he was a good man, a pious man, who believed firmly that God was with him and would preserve him and the family. Years after their wedding, his letters to her when they were separated still left her breathless. "Good-bye, my soul, my little dove, my happiness, joy of my life, I kiss you until I am out of breath." She liked to respond in kind. "My sweetheart, my angel, my only wish is to have you visit me; you know that it's the greatest holiday for me, the greatest pleasure in my life when you're with me."[5]

"Yes, I love him now."

Fyodor felt better. If Mother loved Father, he must be good. She could only love a good man. If she loved him, she made him good. Fyodor thought again about Father's softer side. He had taught the boys to read with a book of Bible stories that communicated his own sturdy Orthodox Christianity, and all the Dostoevsky children knew Christ and the gospels from their earliest childhood.[6] When Fyodor read through the book of Job for the first time, it overwhelmed him with sorrow. It was one of the first books that ever made an impression on him, and he felt that when he read it, he received the seed of God into his heart.[7] Every time he read it, the seed grew, and he felt as if he were gulping down a flood of grace.

Fyodor loved the evenings, after dinner, when Dr. Dostoevsky would take out one of Ann Radcliffe's haunting tales that made Fyodor's hair stand on end. Sometimes Father read from history books or travel writings, and Fyodor imagined traveling in distant lands. Father's demanding educational methods instilled in Fyodor and Mikhail both a love of reading and a passion for theater, art, and poetry. Father taught him to love Pushkin, terrifying him with the tale of the Bronze

Horseman coming to life to chase Eugene through the dark streets of Petersburg, chasing him to his death; moving him to tears with the story of Aleko joining the gypsies out of love for Zemfira or Onegin's sad love for Tatiana; thrilling him with Pushkin's incomparable lyrics. Fyodor would never forget the thrill of watching Schiller's *The Robbers* with his family when he was ten, the very same year his father bought Darovoe. Father gave him the Walter Scott novels that he would devour during one summer at Darovoe.

"Darovoe! We're going to Darovoe!" The word was an enchantment, a magic land from a fairy tale.

"I can't wait to see all the birds and bugs. I saw a hedgehog last year, and squirrels, and I love the smell of dead leaves. And I like the berries too, and I found some mushrooms," Andrey gushed.[8]

"I can't wait to explore Brykovo," Fyodor said out loud.

"Fedya's wood, you mean," Mikhail countered.

Fyodor did not deny that the wood was his. When in Darovoe, the Dostoevskys stayed in a three-room bungalow with a thatched roof and clay walls, nestled in a large and shady linden grove. On the far side of the garden from the cottage in Darovoe was a dense birch wood, gloomy and wild, riddled with ravines. It was thick, verdant, shadowy. Fyodor loved to walk and run there, though the wood filled him with terror as much as it drew him in. He could not think of Brykovo without a shiver, his heart a strange mixture of pleasure, childish curiosity, and terror.[9]

Fyodor snuggled into the carriage seat and watched the fields pass. The first time he came to Darovoe, they were cutting hay. He had watched the long rows of sharp scythes gleaming all together at every sweeping movement of the hay-makers and then disappearing like fiery snakes, just as if they were hiding somewhere, and the grass, cut at the root, flying on one side in dense, thick piles and laid in long, straight furrows.[10]

Darovoe! We're going to Darovoe! he thought dreamily. The words of Pushkin ran through his head, a poem his father had taught him.

> With fainting soul athirst for Grace,
> I wandered in a desert place,
> And at the crossing of the ways
> I saw a sixfold Seraph blaze;
> He touched mine eyes with fingers light
> As sleep that cometh in the night:
> And like a frightened eagle's eyes,
> They opened wide with prophecies.

Then he was asleep.

~

When the carriage lurched to a stop in front of the Dostoevsky home, Fyodor awoke. He carried parcels into the house and helped Mother with the little ones. Then, as soon as he could, he raced across the field toward Fedya's wood, his wood. As he walked along the edge of the forest, it seemed as if someone were calling him in, beckoning him into the darkness, where the smooth stumps of trees were scattered blackly and thickly. It was deathly silent, and he felt an obscure fear at the uncanniness of the spot. Carefully, stealthily, he walked farther in, into the darkness, into the silence.[11]

Suddenly he heard a voice. This was not the forest speaking to him, but a human voice, and when he heard it his blood froze. "Wolf!" it warned. Brykovo was a refuge for snakes, wolves, and other wild animals.

In a frenzy of fear, Fyodor dashed out of the forest and into the field. At the far end of the field was an old peasant plowing. It was Marey, one of the peasants on the Dostoevsky property. Fyodor ran straight for him and stood panting while Marey pulled his filly to a stop.[12]

"I heard a shout . . . Someone just shouted, 'Wolf,'" the boy babbled.

Marey looked around and, seeing nothing threatening, reassured him. "There's no wolf; you're just hearing things."

He stretched out his hand and stroked Fyodor's cheek.

"Never mind, now; there's nothing to be afraid of. Christ be with you. Cross yourself, lad."

Fyodor was too frightened to cross himself. The corners of his mouth were trembling, and this particularly struck Marey. He quietly stretched out a thick, earth-soiled finger with a black nail and gently touched it to the boy's trembling lips.

"Now, now." He smiled with a broad, almost maternal smile. "Lord, what a dreadful fuss. Dear, dear, dear! Here, take a drink." Marey slung the skin of water from his neck and held it to Fyodor's lips. He gulped it down.

At last Fyodor was convinced there was no wolf and that

he had imagined hearing the cry of "Wolf." It had been such a clear and distinct shout. Two or three times before, he remembered, he had imagined such cries (not only about wolves).

"Well, I'll be off now," Fyodor said, making it seem like a question and looking at him shyly.

"Off with you, then, and I'll keep an eye on you as you go. Can't let the wolf get you!" Marey added, still giving Fyodor a maternal smile, "Well, Christ be with you, off you go." He made the sign of the cross over the boy, and Fyodor finally was able to cross himself. He set off, looking over his shoulder almost every ten steps. Marey continued to stand with his little filly, looking after Fyodor and nodding every time he looked around. Fyodor felt a little ashamed at taking such a fright, but he went on, still with a good deal of fear of the wolf, until he had gone up the slope of the gully to the first threshing barn. Here the fear vanished entirely, and the family dog Volchok came dashing out to meet him. With Volchok he felt totally reassured, and he turned toward Marey for the last time. He could no longer make out his face clearly, but he felt that the peasant was still smiling kindly at him and nodding. Fyodor waved, and Marey returned the wave and urged on his little filly.

"Gee-up," came his distant shout, and his little filly once more started drawing the wooden plow.

≈

Fyodor took a sip of his vodka and began to roll another cigarette. Anna was dusting the crumbs off the table into her palm.

"In 1833, Darovoe burned and burned until it was little more than a desert, with charred posts sticking up here and there,"[13] he said, sadness choking his throat. "My parents loaned money to all the families in the village to help them rebuild, and for several years after, Mother took us back to Darovoe for summer vacations and to assist in the recovery. Then regular visits ceased." He lit a match and took a long pull on the cigarette. "I didn't return for forty years."

"But when we visited, they all remembered him," Anna interrupted. "They knew him, even after all those years. They invited us into their cottages and served us tea."[14]

Fyodor spluttered and coughed and set down the cigarette.

"You must love it here in Staraya Russa," Maikov said. "It is far enough from Petersburg and Moscow that you can feel quiet, and you can be near the heart of Russia."

Anna silently nodded her agreement.

"It is like one of your poems!" Fyodor shouted.

Maikov tried to hide his pleasure, but he smiled behind his beard.

"Darovoe left its mark on me. Already while I was exploring the gloomy wood at Darovoe, already when I found comfort in the calloused dirty hand of a peasant, already then I was gathering the raw matter for my novels. I did not know that, but that was what I was doing. I took a thirsty drink from his flagon, and that was one of the first tastes I had of grace."

Fyodor paused and smoothed the white tablecloth. "That tiny and unimportant spot has left a very deep and strong impression on me for the remainder of my life."[15]

WANDERER

Darovoe," Maikov repeated. "That was where your father died."

"Was killed." They had moved out of the dining room into Dostoevsky's work area. Stacks of periodicals covered most of his desk, with a small green expanse of open space for writing. A Chinese-style lamp burned on one side of the table. Maikov settled onto the leather sofa and stroked his beard. Fyodor motioned toward the bronze samovar, but Maikov shook his head and raised his vodka.

"It started when my mother died," Fyodor looked at his hands. "That happened when I was fifteen, just before Father sent me off to the Military Academy. It was terrible."

Maikov waited in silence as Fyodor stared at the ground. Maikov remarked again on the superhuman intensity of his expression. This was the face, these were the eyes, of a biblical prophet.

"It was the bitterest time in my childhood. Doctors kept

coming and going, and relatives, endless relatives, until we were all exhausted by it, and Mother about to die any minute. Father was totally destroyed.[1] Mother was asleep, and just before she died she woke up. She asked for the icon of Jesus, and then she blessed all of us. It was a moving scene, and we all wept.[2] I was devastated, but I wasn't just worried for myself. I felt sorry for our poor father."[3]

Silence descended on the room. Sounds of the summer night came through the window. Maikov waited. Fyodor's eyes were full of tears. "After Mother died, he fared very poorly. He moved to Darovoe, and we started to hear rumors about him. He started drinking heavily and took a mistress. He struggled to make the estate pay, but he did not have much success. One year, there was not a drop of water, not even dew. Heat and winds ruined everything, and the peasants nearly starved.[4] And I treated him abominably. I was at the Academy, and I kept writing and writing and writing him, begging him for money that he could not afford to send. And do you know why I needed money?"

Maikov did not answer.

"Do you know? I needed money because I wanted to buy a shiny new pair of boots or add to my ration of tea or buy a locker for my books. I hated the other cadets. They were all moral midgets. But, oh, I needed to keep up appearances. I needed the approval of those moral midgets, and I drained my father dry for my own vanity. The tears of my poor father burn still in my soul.[5]

"I know he loved us. I know he did. I know how much he sacrificed for us. But there were times when I hated him.

He would be gloomy, ill-humored, more and more angry. He would tell us that we brought no joy to him, no comfort." Fyodor stopped himself. "No, I cannot speak ill of him. I was responsible for everything. He loved us. He was devoted to us, but it was just his character."[6]

Fyodor had begun to cry. "Then he was found dead in the house at Darovoe. He had suffocated. We told everyone that he had died of a stroke, but all through the neighborhood there were whispers that he had been murdered."

"Is that what you think?"

"Perhaps, perhaps. It would not surprise me. He was a hard man, a demanding man. It would not surprise me if he had pushed the peasants one step too far. I have seen it many times. Men bear up under abuse year after year, and then, suddenly, without warning, something explodes. It looks like it happens all at once, but the pressure has been building for a long time. That might have happened. It might have been the peasants . . ." Fyodor trailed off.

Maikov tried to lighten the mood. "So much for the pure soul of the Russian peasant?"

Fyodor's eyes flashed. Maikov had missed badly. "What is that you say? You think that my father's death shows that peasants are corrupted? Well, why shouldn't they be?"

Maikov saw that Fyodor was going into one of his polemical frenzies, and he was worried about getting him too excited, especially tonight. He did not want to be the cause of a fit.

"Have I told you what I saw when I first arrived in Petersburg? I'm sure I have. I was stopped in my journey and up drove this peacock government courier, dressed in yellow and green plumes and a three-cornered hat. He ran into the station, quickly drank some vodka, and then jumped into the next carriage to continue his journey. He had only just sat down when he leaped up and started shouting at the peasant driver and beating him on the neck. He beat and beat and beat and was still beating when the carriage disappeared around a corner. I would wager that that peasant went home that night and beat his wife, just to take revenge on someone for the shame he felt. It was disgusting, and that scene has stayed in my memory all my life. That is the condition of the peasantry, and you want me to blame them when they decide they can't take any more and kill?[7] No, Maikov. We are all responsible. We are all responsible for all."

~

The chill of the Petersburg night cut through Dmitri Grigorovich and Nikolay Nekrasov, but in their excited chatter, they barely noticed. They had been reading the first novel written by their friend and former schoolmate, Fyodor Dostoevsky, and it moved them to tears. They could not wait until daybreak to tell him. *Poor Folk* was a masterpiece, something new in Russian literature.

As friends, they were biased, but they were not the only ones who were impressed by the book. They had news for Fyodor. Vissarian Belinsky, *the* Belinsky, the greatest critic of his generation, the arbiter of Russian literary taste, had read the story. Belinsky had been in Petersburg only a few years, but through his journal *Notes of the Fatherland* and through his unmatched intensity and enthusiasm,[8] he had already launched a revolution in Russian literature. In 1842, Nicolai Gogol had published both his novel *Dead Souls* and his story "The Overcoat," and Belinsky hailed Gogol as the great new talent in Russian letters, doing in Russia what Sand and others were doing in Western Europe. By addressing contested political issues like serfdom and by depicting contemporary social classes, especially the pathetic minor bureaucratic clerks like the hero of "The Overcoat," Gogol was setting a Russian standard for Russian writers.

Now Belinsky, *the* Belinsky, had found another literary star to add to the firmament, perhaps the brightest star of all.

"Did you hear what Belinsky said?" Grigorovich asked.

"Yes, I know! I went to visit him when he was reading the manuscript, and he said that he had not been able to tear himself away from it for almost two days. He told me that the novel reveals such secrets of life and characters in Russia as no one before him even dreamed of. He called it 'the first attempt at a social novel we've had.' Those were his very words!"[9]

"And to think this is our own Fyodor, the military engineer!" Grigorovich laughed. "Even though I saw it with my own eyes, it is still hard for me to believe that he was a military man. He had the most unmilitary demeanor of anyone I know. He was so eccentric, odd, and unnatural. Marching around with that clumsy yet impetuous gait of his; his uniform sitting awkwardly on him, never pressed; carrying his knapsack, cap, and rifle like chains that he was condemned to wear."[10]

"Mikhail told me that the first thing they did when they

arrived in Petersburg was to visit the Pushkin monuments," Nekrasov added. "Mikhail and Fyodor, the Brothers Dostoevsky, soldier-poets both!"

"And spending every possible moment with their books and writing."

"He's always been mad about Pushkin. I think he was disappointed that Pushkin died at the same time as his mother. He wanted to mourn for Pushkin, but he was already preoccupied with his own mother. I think he likes Gogol only because he reminds him of Pushkin. Without 'The Station Master,' Gogol would be completely naked—no 'Overcoat.'"

Pushkin's story "The Station Master" was a small tragedy about Samson Vyrin, the widowed master of a remote post station. Samson's beautiful young daughter, Dunya, calms irate customers, but she later runs away with a Hussar, leaving her father grieving for the rest of his life.

"These poor folk—they are all Vyrins, all of them crushed down beneath the machine of Russia."

Nekrasov nodded. "Fyodor gave us a whole neighborhood of Eugenes, pursued through the night by bronze horsemen!"

"We will carry little Fyodor in our arms through the streets of the city," Grigorovich shouted as the two friends turned the corner to Fyodor's street.

Nekrasov picked up the theme. "We will go before him like John before Christ. 'Here's a little genius just born, whose works will kill off the rest of literature, past and present. Bow down! Bow down!' We will trumpet his name in the streets, in the salons, in everywhere."[11]

"He is our very own prodigy!"

It was four o'clock in the morning when Dmitri and Nikolay reached Fyodor's door. Fyodor was deep in sleep on the other side. Nikolay had a key, and the friends quietly opened the door and crept to Fyodor's bedroom. At a signal, they both shouted their congratulations. Nikolay lit a lamp and pranced around the room lifting it high. Startled and breathless, Fyodor at first covered his head with his blankets, then he tried to spring at them.

"It is us!" Dmitri exclaimed. "It is Dmitri and Nikolay! We have come to hail Russia's latest literary genius."

Slowly Fyodor's heart calmed, and his eyes cleared. He recognized his friends but still could not understand what they were saying.

"We have read *Poor Folk*, and we were both in tears. It is wonderful, wonderful!" Dmitri and Nikolay formed a chorus.

"You . . . you liked it?"

"It is a masterpiece."

"That is not all," Dmitri added with a flourish. He paused and tried to appear sober, even disappointed, but his gaiety showed through. "Belinsky has read it." He paused again.

"*Belinsky?*"

The friends nodded and said nothing.

"And? *And?* What did Belinsky say?"

"He said you are the next Gogol!"

≈

"What I see in *Poor Folk*," Belinsky was saying, "is a novel unlike any other in Russian. It is a simple novel, but that is essential to its genius. You give us some good-hearted simpletons who think that everyone has a duty to love the world, and that loving the world brings extraordinary pleasure. But they are caught in a machine that they cannot understand. The wheel of life with all its rules and regulations runs over them and fractures their limbs and bones without a word. That is all there is. But, along the way, what drama, what types!"[12]

Fyodor sat across the room from Belinsky himself, sipping his tea. He almost pinched himself to make sure he was not dreaming. He hardly knew what to say. To sit with Belinsky and discuss his own novel! It was sheer ecstasy.

"It is Gogol, but it is somehow different from Gogol."

"Yes, yes," Fyodor said, too excitedly. He became embarrassed and tried to calm himself down. "Gogol makes people laugh at the poor clerks who bustle up and down Petersburg streets. I do not want anyone to laugh. I want them to see the humanity of these people that they ignore and despise every day."[13]

Belinsky looked at him curiously. *What an odd, excited young man.*

Fyodor was getting more excited. "I came to this some time ago after seeing a . . . I should call it a vision. I was walking along in this unreal city of ours, this Petersburg, watching people go by, and suddenly a strange thought began to stir in me. I shuddered, and it was as if my heart were flooded in that instant by a hot surge of blood, which had boiled up with the onset of a mighty sensation, hitherto unknown to me. It was as if I had understood at that moment something which, until then, had merely stirred within me but had not been fully comprehended.

It was as if I saw clearly into something new, a completely new world, unfamiliar to me and known only through dark rumors and mysterious signs. I suppose that in that very moment my existence really began. I began to look around me, and suddenly I caught sight of some strange characters. They were all strange, odd figures, completely prosaic, in no sense Don Carloses or Posas, but quite ordinary titular councilors, yet at that same time sort of fantastic titular councilors."[14]

"Yes, we are surrounded by great drama, are we not?" Belinsky paused. "Do you know my favorite passage from your book?"

Fyodor hesitated. "I would be honored if you told me."

"I found the scene with Makar and the button most moving.[15] There he is, called before his superior, before His Excellency himself, and while he is being told of a mistake in His copying, off pops this button, and it hops and skips and rattles and rolls to the feet of his Excellency. Makar is mortified, horrified. He wants to crawl away where he will never be found again. He scrambles for the button, picks it up, and they move on with their business. But when he has dismissed everyone, His Excellency gives a hundred-ruble note to Makar for some new clothes and shakes his hand. He shakes his hand! That is a wonderful scene, so much feeling and truth."

On the street afterward, Fyodor stopped at the corner of the house, looked up at the sky, at the luminous day, at the passersby, and with his whole being felt that a solemn moment had occurred in his life, a decisive change. He felt that something entirely new had begun, something that he had not anticipated even in his most impassioned dreams. *Oh, I will be worthy of that praise; and what people, what people!* Fyodor's brain swirled and burned. *Such men are only to be found in Russia; they are alone, but they alone have the truth; and the good and the true always conquer and triumph over vice and evil. We shall win; oh, to be of them, with them! This is the most wonderful moment in all my life. I feel drunk with my own glory.*[16]

$$\approx$$

"Look at Turgenev," Belinsky said. "I believe he has nearly fallen in love with our Fyodor."

Belinsky's discussion group, known as the Pleiades, was meeting in the Panaev home, and Fyodor had come with Grigorovich and Nekrasov. Turgenev took an instant liking to him, and Dostoevsky felt a similar attraction to the writer.

An aristocrat, talented, handsome, rich, intelligent, well-educated, and twenty-five years old, Fyodor thought. *I have all but fallen in love myself.*[17]

To the others, it was soon evident that Fyodor did not quite fit in. He was a terribly nervous and impressionable person. He was slender, short, fair-haired, with a sickly complexion, and his small grey eyes darted somewhat uneasily from object to object, and his colorless lips were nervously contorted. Though he knew almost all of the guests, he was disconcerted and did not take part in the general conversation. With the appearance of new young writers in the circle, trouble could be caused if they were rubbed the wrong way by Fyodor's irritability and his haughty tone, implying that he was immeasurably superior to them in talent.[18] The Pleiades began to turn on him.

Fyodor's "lover" Turgenev was the first.

"You really should wander about some in Europe," Turgenev said one evening. "It would be instructive to you."

"I have no objection to Europe," Fyodor said. "So long as no one tries to remake Russia in Europe's image."

"Oh, there you are quite wrong. *C'est ne pas vrai*. Being remade in the image of Europe would be the best thing of all for Russia. German society—that especially is the model we should follow, as German literature is our teacher." He stopped for emphasis, knowing that the next comment would be a pin-prick to Dostoevsky. "To be sure, Pushkin is a fine poet, but Russian literature will go nowhere unless we follow European models, the Enlightenment models that are the future."

"Pushkin is the equal of any European poet," Dostoevsky blurted out. He was shaking. "We can learn as much from him as from Voltaire or your Goethe. He is the great poet of the People, as great as any in any language."

Turgenev's dark eyes sparkled, and he ran his hand through his hair in anticipation of the kill. "Tell me, Fyodor, have you read Goethe?"

"Yes, of course. He is a great poet, but I am simply saying . . ."

"And have the Germans read Pushkin?"

"I don't know, but that is not the point . . ."

"Do *Russians* read Pushkin? Other than literary men, that is? Can you find me a single peasant who knows the first thing about Pushkin? 'With fainting soul athirst for grace, I wandered in a desert place'—would they not find that ridiculous nonsense?"

Fyodor abruptly stood. His face was flushed, and he struggled to speak. Nothing came; he felt strangled. As Turgenev leaned back and roared with laughter, Fyodor grabbed his coat and left, slamming the door behind.

"Well, you're the fine one!" Belinsky said when Turgenev stopped laughing. "You latch on to a sick man, you egg him on, as if you didn't know that when he gets worked up he doesn't know what he's saying."

Deep within his heart, too deep for thought, Fyodor vowed that he would one day take his revenge on Ivan Turgenev. *They are all scoundrels eaten up with envy,* Fyodor finally concluded. *Here is one star that will no longer cluster with the Pleiades.*

≈

"Belinsky was ardently attracted to me," Dostoevsky said. "I am not exaggerating. He was a passionate socialist, and he set about trying to convert me to his faith. He began directly with atheism. That was significant, I thought, and revealed his amazing intuition and his unusual capacity to become totally inspired by an idea."

"Did you see the proclamation of the Internationale? Some two years ago. They said precisely the same: 'We are above all an atheistic society.' That's how it began."

Fyodor nodded. "That's the very essence of the matter. That is the essence of socialism, atheism."

"But you were tempted?" Maikov knew the answer.

"Yes, I wandered. I wandered far away. Belinsky knew that the revolution must begin with atheism. Religion provided the moral foundation of the society he was trying to tear apart, and he knew if socialism was going to succeed he had to break up that foundation. Even Renan, when he wrote a book filled with unbelief, even Renan still considered Christ the ideal of human beauty, an unattainable type, never to be repeated in the future. Belinsky looked at Christ and saw a rival.[19] You know, he radically rejected the family, private property, the moral responsibility of the individual."

"Poor Mrs. Belinsky."

"Ahh, no, Maikov. They are all inconsistent, these socialists. Belinsky was a good husband and a good father. Herzen, too, for all his radicalism—he was a family man. They can't live their socialism. They are still men, though they try to be as gods. That should teach them something."

Fyodor folded his hands and leaned back.

"Belinsky—he was the most blessed among men. He had a remarkably tranquil conscience, but he did have moments of sadness, sadness of a special kind."

"Regret?"

"Oh no, not regret. His sadness all came from questions— 'Why not today, why not tomorrow?' In all of Russia there was no one in a bigger hurry. He was a wanderer, a classic Russian type, an Aleko, an Onegin."

"A Russian Ulysses!"

"Yes, and like Ulysses, a reluctant wanderer. He did not

want to wander. He wanted to run and run and run. Once I met him near the Znamensky church at three in the afternoon. He had gone out for a stroll and was on his way home. He pointed to the Nikolaevsky railway station—this was when it was still being built—and he said, 'I often drop by here and take a look at how the construction is progressing. It makes my heart rest a bit easier.' That is what he said—'It makes my heart rest a bit easier to stand and watch the work: at long last we'll have one railway at least.' He said it with passion. That gave him comfort."

"Railway stations."

"That is not Russian! It is barely human! Christ could not hold his attention. But a steaming locomotive—that was his hope. That was his savior."

3

A DESERT PLACE

Anna was at the door. "Can I get anything for you, Fyodor?"

"No, my dove. Thank you, and thank you for a wonderful dinner."

Anna looked worried. "You won't stay up all night, will you? You need to be well rested for tomorrow."

Fyodor smiled. "There you see, Maikov! That is how a true Russian wife behaves. She is always cooing over me as if she were my mother, telling me when to go to bed, when to get up, what to eat."

"And there," Anna said, "is your typical Russian man, nearly sixty and still in need of a mother!"

"Ahh, she knows me all too well. Yes, my dear, I will get enough sleep. I may spend all night working, but my old, old friend here will tire soon enough."

Anna disappeared from the doorway, and the friends looked at one another for a few moments before Maikov resumed the conversation.

"Belinsky was a weak person. He shifted his critical standards with every change of the wind. Now one theme, now another. He did not stick with any of them very long."

"The worst of it was that he insulted Christ. 'God is a sign of human slavery, human self-alienation. The sooner we stop talking of God, the sooner we will become truly human, truly free.' That was Belinsky's idea of freedom. It is not mine."

Fyodor looked across at Maikov. "Belinsky lost faith in freedom, and so he lost faith in the Russian people. If human beings are only mechanical and material, if they lack moral freedom and responsibility, then there is no reason to place any confidence in the common people. Whether he intended to or not, Belinsky taught us all to hate Russia. That I will not accept. Even if peasants killed my father, I will not hate Russia. You see, for me, it is all one, all a single knot: Christ, freedom, Russia. If Christ exists, then we have faith. If Christ exists, we have hope because Christ is still shining in the soul of Russia.

"That is what I believe now, but back then I was confused." His chuckle was humorless and self-mocking. "I was a fool. I wandered out, and I wandered into a desert, and in that desert I nearly lost my life."

≈

Early on a December morning in 1849, the prison guards at the Fortress of Saints Peter and Paul awakened a group of prisoners with the clinking of keys in the locks of their cell doors. Guards herded prisoners out of the fortress into carriages that waited under the spindly spire of the Peter and Paul Cathedral.

The carriage windows were so thickly frosted that the prisoners had to scrape off the ice with a fingernail to see outside. After crossing the Neva from Hare Island into Petersburg, the carriages wound through the streets, past block after block of yellow apartment buildings until they arrived at Semenovsky Square, a desert of newly fallen snow surrounded by troops formed in a square. On the edges stood a crowd of people looking at the prisoners. Everything was silent. It was the morning of a clear wintry day, and the sun, just having risen, shone like a bright, beautiful globe through the haze of the thick clouds.[1]

The prisoners were pulled from the carriages, and they assembled into the Square. They had not seen each other since their arrest in October, and there was a momentary feeling of reunion and celebration. How everyone had changed! Speshnev had always stood out because of his dark good looks, vigor, and flourishing good health. Now, his face was elongated and had a sickly yellow cast to it. Above his gaunt cheeks, his sunken eyes were surrounded by blue circles.[2]

The joy of reunion quickly evaporated as the prisoners noticed a scaffold, twenty to thirty feet high, covered all around with black cloth. On one side were several stakes in the ground. An official called the prisoners to attention and ordered them to line up.

A priest with a cross walked among the prisoners, talking to each individually. "Today you will bear the just decision of your case."

The prisoners were led past some Russian soldiers up the stairs to the scaffolding, where they were split into two groups. They were ordered to remove their hats, and an official announced: "The Field Criminal Court has condemned all to death before a firing squad."[3]

The priest appealed to them: "Brothers! Before dying, one must repent . . . The Savior forgives the sins of those who repent . . . I call you to confession." As he moved down the row of prisoners, he held a cross to them, and every one of them, even Petrashevsky and Speshnev, kissed the cross. Three men—Petrashevsky, Mombelli, and Grigoryev—were roughly taken from the platform and tied to the stakes nearby. A line of soldiers stood opposite, armed and awaiting the order to aim and fire. Soldiers pulled down the prisoners' hats to hide their eyes, but Petrashevsky refused. He stared defiantly back at the firing squad. He wanted to see which one killed him.

Dostoevsky was in the second group of three prisoners, the next group that would be tied to the stakes and shot as soon as the others had been killed and removed to the caskets waiting in a nearby cart.

Fyodor could not be still. "I must tell you of a story I wrote in prison," he whispered to Mombelli, standing beside him.

When he heard the announcement of death, he turned to another prisoner, Durov, and said, "It is impossible. It's not possible that we'll be executed."

To Speshnev, he repeated a line from Victor Hugo's *Le Dernier Jour d'un Condamné* [*The Last Day of a Condemned Man*]: "*Nous serons avec le Christ*" [We shall be with Christ].

The skeptical Speshnev smiled wryly and replied, "*Un peu de poussiere*" [A bit of dust].[4]

≈

"Why don't you say more?" Petrashevsky asked Fyodor one evening earlier that same year, in April 1849.[5]

Dostoevsky looked up at his host. He had been coming to the meetings of the circle for a year but barely knew Petrashevsky. He shrugged.

After his humiliating expulsion from Belinsky's Pleiades, Dostoevsky, desperately lonely, intellectually intense, eager for friendship and debate, wandered from group to group. He became acquainted with Maikov and his brother, a literary critic. Eventually, he wandered into the literary and political set known as the Petrashevsky circle.

"Come, come. There must be a reason," Petrashevsky was saying. "You are a famous novelist, with things to say, full of ideas, and yet you sit and listen and never speak. I think I have only heard you speak twice in all your visits here. Once you gave us your opinion about Turgenev's stories, and another time you expounded on the topic of egoism. But you almost never want to talk about our plans. Come, tell me. What do you think about Speshnev's proposal?"

"I do not adhere to any of the social systems," Fyodor said quietly, but with passion. "I am convinced that any of them would bring with it inescapable ruin, and I am not talking about us but even in France."[6]

"Indeed?"

"Yes. Think of Russia. You all want to bring Western reform into Russia, but it will not work. Russia has its own traditions, its own institutions. Bringing in foreign Western institutions can only be destructive."

"But surely you agree that Russia needs to be reformed."

"Yes, of course," Fyodor said. "Everyone agrees to that. But the reform should not come in like an invading army or be pressed onto Russia like an alien mold. Reform should come from within Russia, built on Russian institutions."

When they met, Petrashevsky was Dostoevsky's age—twenty-six—and worked at the Ministry of Foreign Affairs as a translator. He was well-known as a clown and an agitator. Inspired by French socialists, he attempted to set up a peasant community, but it was burned to the ground as soon as it was begun. Petrashevsky was not discouraged, but he realized that Russia was unprepared for the kind of social experiments he wanted to try. He saw the need to prepare the ground intellectually, and so he gathered a group of like-minded writers and thinkers to his home and began discussing social, cultural, and political questions. During the spring of 1848, the group became more formal, its meetings organized as a debating club. Because the conversations touched primarily on sociopolitical questions, these Petrashevsky evenings interested everyone enormously; they were the only ones of their kind in Petersburg. The gatherings usually continued until two or three in the morning and ended with a modest supper.[7]

Speshnev walked over to listen to Dostoevsky and Petrashevsky. "If you want to hear our friend Fyodor speak with passion, ask him about the serfs. That is the one reform he cares about."

Fyodor glanced at him warily. *Is he mocking me?* he wondered. *Is he going to be another envious Pleiades?*

He remembered the first time he had met Nikolay Speshnev. Dashing, handsome, vain, wealthy, Speshnev had always had an air of danger and secrecy about him. Early on, he had been a Western liberal who was willing to work toward the gradual expansion of freedom in Russia, but he was becoming more and more radical.

He's become a communist, Fyodor reflected. *He told me that he would use any means available to reform Russia, even if the means are violent. And he's trying to rope me in.*

It was true. Speshnev had been studying the young novelist since he first arrived at the Petrashevsky meetings. He had instantly noted Dostoevsky's passion in the fight against serfdom and thought he might make a revolutionary out of him yet. Speshnev had already created an inner group from the Petrashevsky, a group known as the Palm Durov group. They were publishing a series of radical pamphlets that would be printed on a home lithograph. It was all completely illegal, and with censors watching everything, the plan was risky in the extreme. Mikhail Dostoevsky warned his brother not to get involved, and he urged the Palm Durov group to break up. But Speshnev needed Fyodor. The Palm Durov group could pose as a literary society as long as Dostoevsky was there, and under that cover Speshnev could pursue the deeper plots and conspiracies that most delighted him. Speshnev had even persuaded Dostoevsky to try to convince Maikov to join a secret society that would publish pamphlets to spread discontent with the existing order of Russia. Speshnev knew that Dostoevsky was always short of funds and had paid him for his services. With enough money, Fyodor could be won over, of that Speshnev was certain.

Dostoevsky winced as he remembered accepting the money. *He is a tempter. There stands my Mephistopheles!*[8]

"Speshnev is right," Dostoevsky began slowly. "Serfdom is a horror. The idea that one human being can own another human being—it is inhuman, barbaric. It should be eliminated immediately."

"It is going to happen," Petrashevsky said. "Nicholas has already declared that peasants are not property under the law. Belinsky says that it is a prelude to the liberation of the serfs. I believe he is right."

Speshnev shook his head vigorously. "That was 1847. This is 1849, and we mustn't forget that 1848 intervened between them. You have seen what has happened all over Europe. The French set up their 'Second Republic.' There have been demonstrations all over Germany, calling for freedom of the press and freedom of assembly. They want a German national party. Nationalist movements broke out in Vienna among the Hungarians and Slovaks. They want to be free from the Habsburg Empire. I was in Switzerland during the civil war, and that led to a new constitution in 1848. The cantons are now almost completely autonomous. Everything is changing all over Europe. Thrones are toppling, and you can be sure that the Tsar does not want his throne to topple with the rest. He is frightened, frightened of anything that looks or smells like change. Nothing will happen now. Nothing will happen." He paused dramatically. "Unless we make it happen."

Petrashevsky looked sober. "Speshnev, I sometimes wonder if you would stop at *anything* to advance the cause. I wonder."

Speshnev gave him a tight smile.

"Do you know how dangerous your words are?" Petrashevsky continued. "Do you know how much risk you put us all in by saying things like that, by your conspiracies and secrecies? Do you? There are spies everywhere. Everywhere! I shouldn't be surprised to find out that there is a spy among us, a spy here tonight."

Speshnev's dark eyes bored into Petrashevsky. "I know that spies are everywhere. We are in a war, a war to make Russia a just socialist state. We cannot wait until the Tsar becomes accommodating. We must force the issue, especially"—he gestured toward Dostoevsky—"especially regarding the serfs." If he could draw Dostoevsky into a public clash with Petrashevsky, Fyodor might be further radicalized, ready for a more active role in the revolution.

"I believe, of course, that the serfs should be freed. Undoubtedly, that is the only humane and just thing to do," Petrashevsky continued. "But that is not the first thing that must be done. I have been meaning to say this for some time, and I came this evening prepared to make my case. We must free the serfs, but Speshnev is right. That will not happen now, or soon. But that does not mean that we have to wait for all reforms. Other reforms are more achievable, more immediate. Instead of agitating for the freedom of serfs, we should be working to reform the judicial system. Eventually, we will get to the serfs, but freeing the serfs must wait until a better time."

A general cry of protest greeted his argument. Dostoevsky was almost shouting. "We cannot tell the peasants, crushed underfoot by the whole system of Russia, to wait while we tinker with the judicial system. They need our assistance, our rescue, now. They have needed it for centuries, and I for one will not tell them they should wait yet more centuries."

Dostoevsky reached into his overcoat. "Have you read Gogol's *Selected Passages?*" He drew a sheaf of papers from an inner pocket and began unfolding them. A few of the Petrashevskii nodded.

"No one admires Gogol more than I. All of Russian literature has come out from under Gogol's overcoat." A few suppressed snickers met Fyodor's pun. "I cannot, however, agree with what he has written here. He wants us to withdraw from politics. Injustice cannot be solved by politics, he says, but only by the conversion of individual souls."

Speshnev guffawed.

"I have here a letter, a public letter, from Belinsky. It will be published soon. In it, Belinsky calls for the abolition of serfdom and corporal punishment. He says that Gogol is quite wrong to say that Russia needs more sermons and prayers. Russia has already had far too many sermons and prayers, and still the serfs are not free. Russians bow to icons and chant their hymns, and still the serfs are not free. We talk and talk, and still the serfs are not free, still they are lashed like Israel in Egypt. Russia does not need a religious awakening, but a human one. Listen to what Belinsky writes: 'The awakening in the people of a sense of their human dignity lost for so many centuries amid the dirt and the refuse; she needs rights and laws conforming not with the preaching of the Church but with common sense and justice. Instead of which she presents the dire spectacle of a country where men traffic in men, without even having the excuse so insidiously exploited by the American plantation owners who claim that the Negro is not a man.'"[9]

Fyodor was breathless. "I agree with that with my whole heart."

The group went into hysterics.[10] "I must have that letter, Fyodor," Mombelli shouted. "Give me that letter, and I will make copies. Two days from now, it will be plastered all over Petersburg."

It was early morning when Fyodor arrived back at his lonely, unkempt bachelor apartment. Most from the Petrashevsky had stayed all night, including P. D. Antonelli, a recent addition to the circle who was just what the Petrashevsky feared—a government spy—who listened attentively to everyone who spoke, most especially to the young novelist, Fyodor Mikhailovich Dostoevsky.

Reading Belinsky's letter to the group sealed Dostoevsky's fate as far as the secret police were concerned. On April 22, Dostoevsky spent the evening out and returned home in the early hours of the morning. He had barely fallen asleep when he was awakened by a tapping noise in his room. A police officer of the Third Section was standing above his bed. The officer politely told him to dress, and Dostoevsky was taken by carriage to the Fortress of Saints Peter and Paul.

In October, the investigation concluded, and members of the Petrashevsky stood for trial. Dostoevsky admitted that he had been thoughtless but denied that he was subversive. Despite his pleas, fifteen of the group were condemned on November 16 and sentenced to death.

~

Thus Fyodor Dostoevsky, son of a Moscow doctor, graduate of a military academy, rising star of Russian literature, found himself standing in the deepening snow in Semenovsky Square early on the morning of December 22, watching as several of his friends were tied to stakes. He waited with the certainty that he would soon stand at a stake too.

I do not feel the least remorse. Dostoevsky was surprised at the thought. He looked up and down the line of convicts. *All of us think it dishonorable to renounce our convictions. We are all thinking about our meaner actions, but that deed for which we have been condemned, those ideas and those notions which possessed our spirits, we all see as not only requiring no repentance but even somehow as purifying us in a martyrdom for which we will be forgiven much.*[11] Facing death, Dostoevsky felt more alive than ever.

Dostoevsky and the other convicts waited for the order to fire. There were ten dreadful, infinitely terrible minutes of waiting.[12] Then there was a roll of drums. Some of the convicts thought shots would soon fire, but the ex-officer Dostoevsky knew immediately that his life had been spared.[13] The drum roll was a prearranged stand-down signal. A moment later, a soldier rushed into the Square on horseback with a message directly from the Tsar. The decree of execution had been commuted. They were to live; they were to be sent to the living death of Siberia.

Grigoryev collapsed in a heap. He never recovered from the fright and remained a broken man the rest of his life.

Two days later, Fyodor found himself traveling to Siberia. At the station, he said good-bye to his distraught brother Mikhail, whom Fyodor attempted to comfort. As they crossed the Urals, the horses and sledge foundered in the drifts. A snowstorm was raging. They got out of the sledges—it was night—and stood waiting while the sledges were dragged out. All around them, nothing but snow and storm. It was the frontier of Europe and a gateway to the exotic east. Ahead was Siberia and an unknown fate, while all the past lay behind them. It was so depressing that Fyodor was moved to tears.[14]

One of the convicts was contemplating suicide along the way. Dostoevsky pulled some excellent cigars out of his coat and offered one to his fellow prisoner. The two men spent the night in friendly conversation. The other convict was soothed by Dostoevsky's sympathetic, gentle voice, his tenderness and delicacy of feeling; and even some of the capricious sallies had a soothing effect on him. Before the night was out, he had decided against suicide.[15]

≈

Fyodor could hear Anna calling Fedya at the door of the dacha. It was dark, and crickets were chirping.

"Fyodor," Anna said as she came in the door wiping her

hands on her dress. "Can you go out and find Fedya. That son of yours loves to explore, like his father I suppose. It's dark, and he's gone too far to hear me."

"Takes after his father," Maikov said.

"Just a moment," Fyodor said as he stepped through the door into the darkness.

"He's quite devoted to the children," Maikov observed to fill the silence.

"They are dear to him because . . ."

Maikov knew what she was going to say. "I'm sorry. The loss still pains him?"

"Very much."

Fyodor glanced at the two as he came through the door carrying Fedya in his arms. "Here is the little explorer. He was halfway to Borneo, but I convinced him to return for supplies. He'll set out again in the morning." Fyodor hugged his son, kissed his cheeks, and set him down.

"Tomorrow to Borneo!" Fedya said as he ran from the room. Fyodor settled into his chair and rolled another cigarette.

"During our stay at the Fortress, we Petrashevskii were investigated by a Commission of Inquiry, which was headed then by General Nabokov. I was not frightened, but I found the interrogations nerve-racking."

It had been a long day, but Maikov was rapt. He had heard it all before, but what a life his friend had had!

"I evaded questions as best I could so as to avoid revealing more than I should or incriminating anyone else." He sighed. "All my dodges and evasions did no good. I was off to Siberia. I felt like Israel in the wilderness, like Job bereft of all. Going to Siberia was a descent to the grave."

"Such an experience—coming so close to death, being sent to the end of the world—it must have shaken you to the core."

"Standing in the line to be shot, face-to-face with death, it makes you come alive more than anything can. In some odd way, it made us more alive than ever. I wish I could have a gun to my head every moment of my life—I might be a good man then! But it was something else that changed us all, changed those of us who did change."

In the gathering darkness, he sat quietly for some minutes. Something hooted in the woods outside. "When they sent me to Siberia, they sent me off to the People. I was forced into brotherly union with them in a common misfortune. That is why I can honestly say that death in Siberia was one of the best things that ever happened to me."

4

SERAPH'S BLAZE

Those years in Siberia," Fyodor continued. "Those years were horrifying. My first reaction was shock. I was surrounded by people more coarse, ill-natured, and cross-grained than I believed possible. They would have eaten us alive, given the chance. The cold was unbelievable. I spent four hours a day on physical labor, when the mercury froze and there was perhaps about 40 degrees of frost. Prisoners were piled on top of each other in the barracks, and the floor was matted with an inch of filth. Ice froze on the window panes an inch thick, the ceiling dripped, the barracks were draughty. Fleas, lice, and black beetles buzzed and crawled about me by the bushel. It was impossible not to behave like pigs."[1]

He chuckled gloomily. "Somehow we survived, and even got used to it. Man is a creature that can get accustomed to anything, and I think that is the best definition of him."

Maikov shook his head slowly. "I cannot imagine it."

"I was not well either. I had had my first attack of epilepsy a few years before, though at the time I did not know what it was. I suppose I had fooled myself, deceived myself, into thinking that it was not epilepsy. Somewhere in my heart I knew. It was not long before they were a regular occurrence."

Maikov said, "And yet you said a moment ago that you would not exchange the experience for anything in the world. It was the best thing that ever happened."

"It is true. It was a physical shock like nothing I had experienced before, but it was more shocking than that. It challenged everything I had ever thought. No, 'challenge' is too weak. It was a crossroads. No, too weak again. It dismantled me, flayed me, tore me into pieces, killed me, and then made me again. Belinsky made me an atheist, but there in Siberia I found Christ, found Him again. He found me. Siberia was a tree of knowledge. I never saw anything until I had gone to Siberia, nothing at all; my eyes were closed tight. Have I told you what I read while I was in prison?"

Maikov nodded. "I have heard this story."

"Of course. I must be boring you." Maikov shook his head vigorously. "Ahh, well. It deserves repeating, and I am feeling nostalgic. I'll repeat it to myself, and you can listen in! There I was, once the toast of all the literary societies and salons of Petersburg, the new star in the firmament, the new Gogol. There I was, condemned to live with animals for years on end and with nothing to read at all except the New Testament that Natalya Fonvizina was kind enough to bring me. It was the only book permitted in the prison. This book lay under my pillow during the four years of my penal servitude. I read it and sometimes read it to others. I used it to teach one convict to read. She was one of the Decembrist wives, you know."

The Decembrists had organized a feeble protest against autocracy and oppression during the month between the death of Alexander I in November 1825 and the coronation of Nicholas I early the following year. They marched into the Senate Square calling for the establishment of a constitutional monarchy under the leadership of Nicholas's brother, Constantine. Crying "Constantine and konstitutsiya," they marched into a massacre. Several were killed on the spot, five of the leaders were hanged shortly after, and several dozen more were exiled to Siberia for life. Their wives heroically followed them, settling in the villages near the prison camps.

"She gave up everything, position, wealth, connections, family ties. She sacrificed it all. She was completely innocent, and for twenty-five years she bore everything that her husband bore."

Maikov nodded again. "She was one of the sublime sufferers,"[2] he said. "Like you."

"No, no, no. I did not suffer patiently, and I did not sacrifice as she did. But my suffering did teach me about sacrifice. Natalya, and many others, taught me what it meant to sacrifice."

Maikov took a sip of vodka.

"Natalya gave me life when she gave me that book," Fyodor was saying. "I was in the house of the dead, and she gave me life."

≈

The courtyard of the prison that greeted the new inmates was large, two hundred paces long and a hundred and fifty wide, in the form of an irregular hexagon, all shut in by a fence of high posts stuck deeply into the earth. Inside the fence was a world apart, unlike everything else, with laws of its own, its own dress, its own manners and customs. Here was the house of the living dead.[3]

Here were men unlike any that Fyodor had ever encountered. He was surrounded by murderers, thieves, parricides, brigands. They drank heavily, quarreled incessantly, fought with horrible brutality. They remained thieves in prison, and Dostoevsky was a victim. Prostitutes, male and female, snuck in and out to service prisoners and guards. Gather all the criminals, confine them in a small space in harsh conditions—prison does not produce saints.

There was Petrov, a fearless and determined man. One day, he was summoned by the major in charge of the prison to answer for some wrong. He turned pale when his name was called. As a rule, he lay down to be flogged resolutely and without a word, endured his punishment in silence and got up again quite lively, looking calmly and philosophically at the mishap that had befallen him. He was always, however, handled with caution. But this time, for some reason, he thought himself in the right. He turned pale and managed, unseen by the guard, to slip into his sleeve a sharp English knife. Knives and all sharp instruments were strictly forbidden in prison.

All the convicts rushed to the fence and looked through the crevices with beating hearts. They all knew that this time Petrov did not mean to lie down to be flogged and that it would be the end of the major. But at the critical moment the major got into his droshki and drove away, leaving the execution of the punishment to another officer. As for Petrov, he bore his punishment quite calmly. His wrath passed off with the departure of the major.[4]

There was the large prisoner, a brutish Tartar named Gazin. Gazin drank heavily, and as he drank he became violent. Eventually he passed into a stage of blind fury, snatched up a knife, and rushed at people. At first, the other convicts ran from him, but eventually they found another, more effective solution. A dozen men, inmates of the same prison ward as Gazin, would rush at him all at once and begin beating him. They beat him on the chest, on the heart, on the pit of the stomach, on the belly. They beat him hard and beat him a long time; they only desisted when he lost consciousness and lay like a corpse. They could not have brought themselves to beat any other convict like that. To beat like that meant killing any other man, but not Gazin. Then they wrapped his unconscious body in a sheepskin and carried it to the bed.

"He'll sleep it off," one of his fellow inmates would say, and he did. For several years, every time he got drunk, it ended the same way, in a savage beating. Still he got drunk. In the end, though, the beatings took their toll. "He is breaking up!" the other convicts said as he began to complain about aches, got weaker, and spent more time in the hospital.[5]

Most chilling was Orlov, who had been a famous robber, a runaway soldier before capture and imprisonment. Excitement spread through the prison when the other convicts learned that Orlov was to join them. When he arrived, he was unconscious, pale, his back swollen and red and blue. The next day, he amazed everyone by regaining consciousness and walking around the hospital. Though small and weakly built, he was the strongest man in the prison. In other brigands, it was obvious that the flesh had so completely gained the upper hand of all spiritual characteristics that at the first glance, you could see from their faces that nothing was left but a fierce lust of physical gratification—sensuality, gluttony. Not so Orlov. He was unmistakably the case of a complete triumph over the flesh. It was evident that the man's power of control was unlimited, that he despised every sort of punishment and torture and was afraid of nothing in the world. The other prisoners saw in him nothing but unbounded energy, a thirst for action, a thirst for vengeance, an eagerness to attain the object he had set before him. He looked down on everything with incredible disdain, though he made no sort of effort to maintain this lofty attitude—it was somehow natural.[6]

Presiding over the inmates was a man no less depraved than his charges, the sadistic Major Krivtsov. The major was, so to speak, a fateful being for the prisoners; he had reduced them to trembling before him. He was insanely severe and flew at people. What they feared most in him was his penetrating lynx-like eyes, from which nothing could be concealed. He seemed to see without looking. As soon as he came into the prison, he knew what was being done at the farthest end of it.

The prisoners called him "eight eyes." Krivtsov's cruelty was not always physically painful. He would burst into a barracks at night, awakening everyone with the announcement that anyone who was caught sleeping on his left side would be flogged, since Christ required men to sleep only on their right sides. Krivtsov was eventually tried for his abuses and removed from the prison.

≈

"The major's methods will not work," Dostoevsky whispered to fellow prisoner Akim Akimitch at dinner one evening. "By his ferocious, spiteful actions he only exasperated people who are already exasperates, and if he was not under the governor of the prison, a generous and sensible man who sometimes moderates his savage outbursts, his rule might lead to great trouble."[7]

"That kind of talk will make you his next target," Akim answered gruffly.

Fyodor tore his piece of bread and dipped half of it into the unidentifiable liquid on his plate. "I would think he'd want the prisoners to be compliant, cooperative."

"That is not what he wants. He wants resistance so he has an excuse to beat us even harder."

Fyodor weighed the theory as he took a sip of tea. The notion that human beings act more out of spite and hatred than out of love and a desire for peace was becoming more and more persuasive to him.

"You know," he said, trying out one of his own theories. "In the time I have been here, I have seen not the slightest trace of repentance, not one sign that the prisoners' crimes weigh heavily on their consciences."

"Well, most of them consider themselves to be completely in the right. This is a fact."

"Yes, that is true. But I wonder where that comes from. Why would they be so reluctant to admit they were wrong? Why should they be so resistant to the truth? Vanity, bad examples, foolhardiness, and false shame are the causes of much of it, no doubt."

Akim chewed slowly. *I wonder if he understands a word I am saying,* Fyodor thought, then pressed on. "But here is what I have come to. The human heart is desperately wicked, twisted, unfathomable. Crime cannot be comprehensible from the points of view that are already given, and its philosophy is rather more difficult than is commonly supposed."[8]

"Philosophy of crime," Akim laughed. "That is a good one, that is. You intellectuals. You think everything has to be turned to philosophy. There is no philosophy. There are just crimes and criminals. When you go back to Petersburg and start writing again, you can write a book on it. *The Philosophy of Crime*, by Fyodor Dostoevsky. Everyone will think you are a genius, they will."

"Perhaps I shall," Fyodor said to himself.

～

"Clear out. Here comes Gazin."

Gazin was drunk, and that meant unpredictable. Fyodor tried to avoid his stare, but Gazin was coming straight for him.

"So you've money, have you?" he roared. "So you've a lot of money, eh? Have you come to prison to drink tea? You've come to drink tea, have you? Speak, damn you!"

Dostoevsky and Akim remained silent, and Gazin's anger boiled hotter. Near him in the corner stood a big tray that was used for slices of bread cut for the meals of the convicts. It was large enough to hold the bread for half the prison; at the moment it was empty. He picked it up with both hands and raised it above them. In another moment, he would have smashed their heads.

Fyodor looked around him frantically. *Not one word in our defense!* He was seething himself now. *Not one shouts at Gazin. Why, they seem pleased at our position. They want him to flatten our heads with the tray.*[9]

Gazin was about to let fly the enormous tray, which he was turning and twisting above his head, when a convict ran in from the barracks and cried out, "Gazin, they have stolen your vodka!"

The horrible brigand let the tray fall with a frightful oath and ran out of the kitchen. "Well, God has saved them," said the prisoners among themselves, repeating the words several times.

When his heart started beating again, Dostoevsky turned to Akim. "Why does he hate me so?"

"They are not fond of gentlemen," he said after a moment. "Especially politicals. They are ready to devour you, and no wonder. To begin with, you are a different sort of people, unlike them. Besides, they've all been serfs or soldiers. Judge for yourself whether they would be likely to be fond of you."[10]

Akim's words cut through Fyodor like a knife. Since meeting Belinsky, he had entertained the naïve hope that there could be a convergence of intellectuals and peasants in Russia. The peasants were waiting patiently, eagerly, for leadership from the Belinskys and Dostoevskys of Russia. In their simple way, they would trust their betters. They had no concept of social status anyway, the simple souls. Now Fyodor knew it was all a lie. Peasants had as much social sensitivity as he did, probably more, and they were certainly not looking for Petersburg intellectuals to come riding in on white horses to save them.

Fyodor knew now that it was a lie, and he hated the peasants for it. They hated him, and he hated them back, with all the intensity he could muster.

≈

It was Easter Sunday. Surrounded by quarreling prisoners, wishing for a little solitude, Fyodor got disgusted and went for a walk. When he passed one of the Polish prisoners, Mirecki, the Pole whispered, *"Je haïs ces brigands"* (I hate those brigands). Dostoevsky realized that Mirecki had given voice to his own hostility. When he returned to his bunk, he recalled the incident with the peasant Marey many years before. Suddenly he felt he could regard these unfortunates in an entirely different way and that, through some sort of miracle, the former hatred and anger in his heart had vanished.

He peered intently into the faces of the others in his room. *This disgraced peasant, with shaven head and brands on his cheek, drunk and roaring out his hoarse, drunken song—why he might also be that very same Marey; I cannot peer into his heart, after all.*[11]

Over the next few days, he continued to observe the other prisoners, and he began to see that, underneath the hardness and cruelty, or mixed with it, there was some residual decency. They treated an Old Believer in the camp with respect, recognizing that he was a saint. The following Christmas, they asked Fyodor to help organize a vaudeville show.

For their depravity, Dostoevsky began to see, as if a seraph had touched his eyes, that there was something good there, and he took this as a sign of the continuing presence of Christ in their souls.

~

"What man needs most," Dostoevsky told Akim one afternoon as they put their shovels away, "is freedom."

"Then we lack what we need most."

"Not entirely. Even here, even the house of the dead, there are little signposts of freedom. We enjoy our freedoms too."

Akim looked skeptically at his friend.

"You've noticed yourself how obsessed prisoners are with money. You have told me this. They are morbidly, insanely greedy of money."

Akim pulled off his gloves and waited. "More philosophy, I suppose. Go on. I am listening."

"But then what do the prisoners do when they get money?"

"They burn it all. They spend it immediately on drink, on women, gambling."

"There you see, just as I said." Fyodor was beaming. His hands were spread out as if he had just completed a laboratory experiment that conclusively proved that lead could be turned to gold.

Akim shrugged.

"Don't you see? When they get money, they throw it away like so much rubbish. That's the way it looks. But they are spending their money on something of more value. What is more precious than money for the convict? Only one thing. *Freedom* or some dream of freedom. By spending money, he is showing a will of his own. In spite of brands, fetters, and the hateful prison fence that shuts him off from God's world and cages him in like a wild beast, he is able to obtain vodka. He can persuade himself, if only for a time, that he has infinitely more power and freedom than is supposed."

"Money is coined liberty?"[12] Akim said, proud of his wit.

"Yes, that's it. That is it exactly." Fyodor was almost giggling. "Coined liberty. That's good, very good."

Akim beamed, pleased at Fyodor's pleasure.

"I tell you," Fyodor said in great excitement, "freedom is, the mainspring of human action. I have been watching carefully all this time, watching men who have little freedom, men who have been imprisoned because of terrible crimes. But even here, I see that everything is about freedom. Why, for instance, do we not rebel against the tedium of the camp? What keeps us here? Why are we not at each other's throats every night?"

Akim shrugged again.

"It is work."

"The work is boring. It drives me mad."

"Yes, the official prison work does. If that were all we had, we would go mad. If you wanted to crush, annihilate a man utterly, you could do it by assigning him meaningless, endless labor—pounding sand to no purpose, moving earth from here to there and back again. But that is not all we do here. Each of us can work on his own. The authorities officially don't allow it, but the guards wink at it. Because we have craft work, we all have an outlet to exercise freedom in labor and to achieve a certain measure of dignity. We have something to call our own, a place where we are free."

"For a prisoner, you talk a lot about freedom."

"What else is there to talk about here, in this grave? If I did not think about freedom, I would die with all the other dead who are here."

Fyodor and Akim trudged across the frozen ground toward their quarters. The wind was howling, and Fyodor pulled the collar of his ragged coat over his face. Behind the coat, his voice was muffled, but he kept talking.

"I believe even crime is an expression of freedom."

"Yes, I suppose so. I was free to steal, and so I was imprisoned."

"Oh, that is too simple. Yes, there are those who think they can demonstrate how free they are by ignoring moral rules, but that is not what I mean. Think of a fire heating water to steam. The water gets hotter and hotter, and the steam more and more angry. If the steam doesn't have anywhere to go, the whole thing will explode. That is crime. When normal channels for the expression of human freedom and dignity are closed off, people look for other channels. No wonder our people are so full of violence. We bottle them up and turn up the heat, and then we are surprised when they explode."

Fyodor paused, slightly breathless. He coughed. "But that's not all. It's not just freedom. It's about beauty too."

"Criminals are artists! I like that. Maybe I can get some of my crimes into a gallery." Akim pursed his lips and tiptoed daintily. "I am an artiste of crime!"

Fyodor smiled and went on. "Have you ever seen how a peasant beats his wife? I have. He begins with a rope or a strap. He grows heated and finds it to his taste. At last he grows wild, and his wildness pleases him. The animal cries of his victim intoxicate him like liquor. Suddenly, he throws down the strap. Peasant life is without aesthetic pleasures such as music, theaters, and magazines. It is natural that a peasant would fill this void with something. He fills it with a pleasant night of drink and beating."[13]

"You are insane, Fyodor, insane."

"No, no. They want what everyone else wants. But their desires get twisted and turned and they seek satisfaction in perversions. At bottom, they are like everyone else. They are human and have human motives. They want freedom and beauty. It all comes back to Christ. When your eyes are opened, that's what you see, that it all comes back to Christ."

Akim looked at him skeptically.

"Yes, Christ. Christ is the ideal, the ideal of beauty, the ideal of freedom. Lose Him, and we have nothing, nothing but money and drink and crime . . ."

"And peasants torturing their wives for pleasure?"

"Yes, exactly that."

"You are insane, Fyodor. Insane."

≈

"Siberia regenerated your sacred feeling of love for the father-land. Prison camp works! You come back loving the hand that beats you.[14] I can see that going to the house of the dead will knock the socialism out of you." Maikov sipped his vodka.

"You misunderstand me. I came out even more intensely concerned about justice, about the evils of Russia. It was far more obvious to me than ever, as if I had been squinting at something very fuzzy and vague and suddenly my eyes were opened wide. I became even more convinced that our system must be changed. Listening and watching all those years, I became convinced that crimes cannot be compared even approximately. Two men commit murders; all the circumstances of each case are weighed; and in both cases, almost the same punishment is given. Yet look at the difference between the crimes. One may have committed a murder for nothing, for an onion; he murdered a peasant on the high road who turned out to have nothing but an onion. Another murders a sensual tyrant in defense of the honor of his betrothed, his sister, or his child. Another is a fugitive, hemmed in by a regiment of trackers, who commits a murder in defense of his freedom, his life, often dying of hunger. These are not the same crime at all. Yet all of these are sent to the same penal servitude."[15]

Dostoevsky paused. "But that is not the deepest lesson of

Siberia. The deepest lesson was about Christ, about Christ and Russia. Europe and her mission will be realized by Russia. This has been clear to me for a long time."

"You have more hope than I do, Fyodor. The Russian people know the gospel poorly, and they do not know the fundamental principles of our faith. They know nothing."

"Yes, yes, you are quite right. I grant that. But they do know Christ, and they have borne Him in their hearts from time immemorial. There can be no doubt of that. Perhaps the only love of the Russian people is Christ, and they love His image in their own fashion, to the point of suffering. And they take pride in the name Orthodox. The people are convinced that the Orthodox conception of Christ is truer than any other. Ask a Russian, and he won't be able to tell you the first thing about the Orthodox Christ, but still he knows that Orthodoxy exists to preserve Him. There is much one can know unconsciously."[16]

Fyodor sat silently for a few moments.

> I saw a sixfold Seraph blaze;
> He touched mine eyes with fingers light
> As sleep that cometh in the night:
> And like a frightened eagle's eyes,
> They opened wide with prophecies.

"You cannot judge the Russian people by the abominations they commit, but by those great and sacred things for which, even in their abominations, they constantly yearn. Not all the people are villains; there are true saints, and what saints they are; they are radiant and illuminate the way for all. But even for those who aren't saints, look deeper. Open your eyes wide, Maikov; open your eyes. Do not judge our people by what they are, but by what they would like to become. I tell you that Christ still lives in the Russian soul. Christ is hard to see, but He is still there. I tell you, He hasn't abandoned our people."[17]

5

TUMULT AND ROARING SOUND

Fyodor! What is happening, Fyodor?! What is happening?"

Frantic, Marya Dostoevsky leaped to her husband as he fell to the ground. He yelped like a wild beast. Foam flecked his mouth, his face twisted in inhuman contortions, his body convulsed and twitched, tightened, loosened, and twitched again.

A moment before, he had been sipping champagne and telling Count Peter stories about his imprisonment. Then he collapsed.

"Won't someone help? Please, please help him. I beg you." Her own voice sounded strange to her.

Their host, Count Peter Semenov, was already at the door wearing his hat and cape. "Keep him calm, Marya. Try to keep him calm. I will return with the doctor in a moment."

Marya knelt helplessly beside him, trying to quiet his heavy

59

breathing. "Fyodor, Fyodor. My husband, my husband. What is happening to you? What will happen to us?"

It was an inauspicious beginning to a honeymoon, but then, Marya reflected, the entire romance had been inauspicious from the start.

≈

When they met, Marya Dimitrievna Isaev was already married to Alexander Ivanovich Isaev, who had moved to Semipalatinsk to take a position as a customs official. Fyodor met her through the family of Lieutenant-Colonel Belikhov. With his early Petersburg literary celebrity, Dostoevsky secured a position as tutor to several schoolchildren in Semipalatinsk and would often visit Belikhov to read to him. Through that connection, he became acquainted with the upper class of provincial society, including the Isaevs.

As she stroked the head of her convulsing husband, Marya remembered how many days Fyodor had spent in her home teaching her son, Pasha. She was energized by his intellectual energy, and she pitied his many physical ailments. She looked forward to his visits more and more, and Fyodor, never one to hide his feelings, declared his love for her with overwhelming enthusiasm.

When Marya's husband took a new post in Kuznetsk, a post even more obscure than that in Semipalatinsk, Dostoevsky was devastated. He borrowed money from his German-Russian friend Wrangel—dear Wrangel!—to help them make the move. Fyodor and Wrangel accompanied the departing family over the first stage of their journey, and while Wrangel filled Alexander Isaev with wine, Fyodor and Marya snuck away to a carriage to say good-bye.

"I have never considered our meeting as an ordinary one, and now that I will be deprived of you, I have understood many things," Fyodor had said. From another man, it would have sounded like a prepared, melodramatic speech. But Fyodor filled everything he said with his whole soul. "I lived for years deprived of human beings, alone, having nobody, in the full sense of the word, to whom I could pour out my heart. The simple fact that a woman held out her hand to me has constituted a new epoch in my life."

His eyes burned as he paused. Marya could not bear to look at him.

"You have brought me new life. In certain moments, even the best of men, if I may say so, is nothing more or less than a blockhead. The heart of a woman, her compassion, her interest, the infinite goodness of which we do not have an idea and which often, through stupidity, we do not even notice, is irreplaceable. I found all that in you."[1]

It all came back to her now. The moonlit night, the breathless rush to the waiting carriage, the breathless rush of words. Marya still marveled at her daring. *Sneaking around my husband, it was so thrilling. It was so painful,* Marya thought. *God is punishing us for our love. God is punishing us for not waiting.*

Marya hoped that the move would cool Fyodor's love, but it had the opposite effect. Letter after letter arrived, and she responded to each. Fyodor could be a tidal wave, sweeping everything along with him, crashing against every objection. But his letters were as pitiful as they were passionate, and Marya was as sympathetic for his loneliness as she was sick for his love.

≈

The doorknob rattled and the door opened, letting a gust of frigid February wind blow in. Count Peter pushed the door closed and removed his hat. "The doctor is coming. He will be here very soon. How is he?"

"Better. His breathing is slower, and he has stopped convulsing." Marya's own heart was calming down. She was beginning to think that he might survive. "What is wrong with him? Do you know?"

Count Semenov shook his head. "I have never seen it, but I have heard of similar things happening to those with the falling sickness."

"Epilepsy?" Marya let the word sink in. *Is this what I have in store for me? Is this my husband's life?* she thought.

"I will put on some tea."

Marya felt the guilt welling up in her again. She had been so cruel to her husband, even crueler to Fyodor. The letters, oh the letters. Soon after moving to Kuznetsk, she had found another lover, Nikolay, a schoolmaster, who gave her an escape from the drunken stupors of her pathetic husband. That by itself would have broken Fyodor's heart. But the letters, oh the letters. She had written to Fyodor praising her new lover's kindness, nobility, devotion, knowing full well that it would tear Dostoevsky apart with gloom and jealousy.[2]

She had killed her husband, Alexander; of that she was sure. She had scolded and berated him; she had sought out other men. His own failures had driven him to drink, but she had pushed him further, pushed him over the edge.

The letters, oh the letters! Asking Fyodor for romantic advice. "Shall I marry Nikolay? He's young, a good man, in civil service, with an assured future."[3] She might as well have written, "You, Fyodor, are old, unreliable, without a future." He must have been struck by lightning. He must have staggered, fainted, wept all night." Fyodor had told her of his dreams, his night panics, the spasms in his throat choking him, tears that would not come, then came in torrents. And she caused it all.[4] Perhaps even then he was already suffering from epilepsy.

Fyodor had gone to great lengths not only to gain Marya's love but also to arrange his life so he could afford a transfer to the civil service, as well as marriage to her. "I did it for you, you know. I did it all for you," he insisted, and she believed him.

By the end of the year, she consented to marry him. They married on February 7, 1857. That was only days ago, and now her husband lay unconscious on the floor of Count Semenov's home. They had not even returned home yet.

≈

A sharp knock on the door made her start. Count Peter opened the door, and the doctor squeezed in, trying not to let the wind blow snow into the house. He quickly removed his overcoat, knelt down beside Marya, and opened his bag. He felt Fyodor's head, pulled back his eyelids with a cold thumb, and felt for his pulse. He looked sympathetically at Marya.

"Have you seen him have an attack like this before?"

She shook her head.

"I am sorry for you," he said, trying to deepen the sympathy of his look. "It is very frightening. And so soon after your wedding . . ."

Marya said nothing and only looked down at Fyodor's face. His eyes fluttered and then opened. He looked up at Marya. At first, there was no recognition, then the fire lit in his eyes.

"Marya." His voice was weak and hoarse. "What has happened to me? Where are we?"

"We are at Count Peter's. We're staying with him. Don't you remember?"

"Why?"

"We are on our way home. Home to Semipalatinsk."

"We?" He paused and closed his eyes. His mouth worked as if he were chewing. "We?" he whispered again. "We? Home?"

"Yes, Fyodor. Don't you remember? We are married."

6

LIES AND IDLE RUST

Anna had been sitting on the sofa, listening quietly and sewing as Fyodor and Maikov reminisced and talked of their long friendship. In the other room, their daughter Lyubov was getting ready for bed.

"I was ill, with epileptic attacks more and more frequent. I suppose they started much earlier, but no one knew what it was. My ears were filled with tumult and roaring sound, like an earthquake, like the flight of angels crashing around me, in my head. Sometimes I thought I could hear and sense everything all at once, monsters swimming silent in the sea, sap in the tree."

"It must be horrible to work when your head is full of strange noises."

"It is, but that wasn't the only plague. Everyone was after me even before I returned to Petersburg. It was the December 1855 issue of *The Contemporary*. I will never forget it. I can still see the page. 'He could not maintain himself at the height on which we had placed him'—that is what they wrote about me."

"Icarus!" Maikov cried. "You had flown too high, too soon. You created convulsions in the sky, and so you had to come crashing down to earth."

"Nonsense," Anna broke in. "They know nothing. They were only envious of you, secretly glad to see you packed off to Siberia while they continued to live with their Petersburg comforts."

Fyodor shrugged. "Envy was only part of it. It was something more. They were traitors."

"Yes, and look what it got them," Anna said. She was excited. "Look at where you have come. Where are all these men? Where is Nekrasov now? Will he be there at the festival? Even if he is, he will not be where you will be, my Fyodor."

Maikov laughed.

Fyodor crossed to Anna's chair, bent down, and gave her a small kiss on the head. "My dove. You will not betray me, will you?"

She looked at him. "If I had a mind to write satires of my husband, I would have much to satirize." Maikov chuckled again. "Nekrasov knew nothing. He had no idea what an odd creature you are, Fyodor. No idea whatever."

A few minutes later, Anna collected her sewing and stood. "I need to get things ready for the night. I do not have the luxury of sleeping until afternoon, as you literary men do. But, Fyodor, do be mindful. You must get some sleep. Tomorrow . . ."

"Yes, my dove. Tomorrow. I will sleep."

When Anna left, Maikov looked at Dostoevsky. "She is a strong woman. She is the perfect woman for you."

Fyodor agreed. "I have always found strong women attractive. I would not want a woman I could completely roll over, though of course I try to roll over all of them, flatten them down in front of me. But they all fight back. That is what makes it enjoyable."

The image of Marya returned to his mind. "My first wife, Marya. She was very strong, too, you remember."

"I do. I remember something of a shrew."

"Ahh, no . . . no. I was suffocating, so demanding. She was a good and tender creature, always noble and good. But she was often angry, very excitable. Her impressions would change with incredible rapidity. When she became angry, it was because she so completely hated injustice of any kind."[1]

"The two of you were made for each other. Two hysterical people under one roof."

Dostoevsky shook his head. He spread out his hands feebly. "All circumstances were against us. We were always short of money. I had just come from prison and did not know how I was going to make a living, except writing, which barely paid. I had to get her son Pasha into the Siberian Corps of Cadets, raise money for a move back to Petersburg, and for a home, and everything. I did not do justice to her. Perhaps she would have been better with Nikolay."

There was something between the two old friends that neither mentioned. A thought, a memory, a ghost haunted the conversation. Maikov hesitated to speak, but Fyodor knew what he was thinking.

"Perhaps we would have both been better off without . . ."

Silence fell between them, until Maikov named the ghost. "Suslova."

≈

Apollinaria Suslova adjusted her hat, looked in the mirror, and frowned. *He will not like it. He is always so critical.* She smoothed the hair beneath the hat, ran a finger over her eyebrows, and pursed her lips as if kissing herself.

He plays the part of a serious, busy man who understands his obligations after his own fashion uncommonly well, she mused. *He is so serious, so ascetic. I suppose he might agree to have some pleasure, if some great doctor or philosopher once said that it was necessary to get drunk every month.*[2]

She would find him working, distracted and working, she was sure of that. *He works round-the-clock and quits his desk only to sleep. Working or sleeping. He always writes at night, he tells me, when there is nothing to distract him, then sleeps from daybreak to mid-afternoon. What an odd, odd man he is.*[3]

She pulled off the hat, tried on another, more to her satisfaction. Adjusting her dress, she pulled a coat over her shawl and buttoned it to the neck before stepping from her apartment onto the frigid Petersburg sidewalk. She turned left and made her way toward Mikhail's apartment where Fyodor would be with the staff of his journal, *Time*.

≈

It was the winter of 1862. Dostoevsky had been back in Petersburg since the end of 1859. His return trip was life from the dead. When he had crossed the Urals on his way into exile, the weather had been frigid and blustery. It was summer when he returned, and he stopped to sip orange brandy with the coachman. He arrived in Petersburg in December, settled in with the help of his brother Mikhail, and got to work writing *Notes from the House of the Dead*, an account of his experience in prison camp.

He wanted nothing more than to return to the height of literary celebrity he lost when he went to Siberia, Apollinaria thought as she bent against the wind. "He did it, and more. Everyone reads what he writes."

The book began serialization in the autumn 1860 issue of *The Russian Word* and was later completed in the Dostoevskys' own journal. *House of the Dead* brought Dostoevsky even more fame than *Poor Folk*.

During the year before Fyodor's return to Petersburg, Mikhail had been making plans to launch a new literary journal. With the ascent of a new Tsar, censorship laws and enforcement had relaxed, and a new burst of freedom had buoyed the Russian press. Mikhail and Fyodor hoped to make the best of the opportunity with a periodical that would be readable, sharp, fiery, energetic, and firm.

Money is always the problem with him, Apollinaria thought. *He always complains that other critics are getting rich from literary journals, even though they are nothing but peasants about literature.*[4]

"I am seeking a middle way," he told Suslova the first time they met. "I am not a Slavophile, because I do not reject

European ideas simply because they are European. But the Slavophiles do have something right. Russia has to be Russia, and not something else. The Russian idea will be the synthesis of all those ideas which Europe had developed, with such persistence and courage, in each of its nationalities; then perhaps everything antagonistic in these ideas will find reconciliation and further development in Russian nationality.[5] I want to give voice to the Russian idea. I want my tongue to speak the truth in all its sheen and shine, no rust."

The Dostoevskys' journal, *Time*, made its first appearance in January 1861.

"Which Russians?" said Fyodor. "Here you live in Petersburg surrounded by books and literate conversation. What about the Russians who cannot read at all?"

"*Pochvennichestvo*—synthesis—that is the key," he shouted with excitement. "We must fuse the interests and talents of cultivated intellectuals with traditional Russian institutions, habits, faith, and morals. That is the middle way."

For several years, *Time* relentlessly, doggedly held out this vision. It was published out of Mikhail's cramped office. Apollinaria Suslova, daughter of a freed serf, well-educated, as strong-willed as her sister who became the first woman in Russia to receive a medical degree, twenty-three years old, was one of the contributors. Soon, she became a lover to one of the editors.

The milky, late-afternoon sunlight was fading as Apollinaria turned the corner toward Mikhail's apartment.

Fyodor listens to the radicals, even though he's not one of them,

Apollinaria thought. *It's because they are young, and he loves children. He's nearly a child himself, sometimes.*

She recalled how Fyodor had taken aim at the Russian aristocrats, the superfluous men, those high-minded Westernized aristocrats who believed that Russia was too backward to provide them with an opportunity to use their talents and who retreated into an aimless literary culture. Dostoevsky wrote that they had plenty of opportunities to use their skills and education: teach a child to read, he urged. He knew that they would consider this beneath their dignity, but that only exposed the more fundamental problem: their unwillingness to sacrifice themselves in a Christlike fashion for the sake of other Russians. "Sacrifice everything, even your grandeur and your great ideas, for the general good: stoop down, stoop down, as low as the level of a child," urged Fyodor.[6]

≈

Fyodor was slouched in a chair with a newspaper when she walked in. Mikhail acknowledged her presence with a slight nod and went back to work editing a manuscript. She stood quietly for some moments, then Fyodor glanced at her.

"Apollinaria! When did you get here? Get out of those wet things, come to the fire. It's terribly cold, terribly." He bustled to her like a Jewish mother and helped her from her coat. He almost shoved her into the seat closest to the fire.

He slapped the newspaper with the back of his hand, stood and paced the room. Mikhail, used to his rants, kept busy with the manuscript.

"Let them travel for a bit in Europe. Let them travel a bit there and get a taste of European decadence, its lies and idle rust." His face reddened as he paced the room. "The Frenchman is pleasant, honest, polite, but money is everything. No trace of any ideal. In the end, the French are simply nauseating.[7] And London! London! I had never before seen a city of Baal. Everywhere the waste of greed and uncharitableness. I spent some time among the prostitutes in the Haymarket. Little girls around twelve years of age take you by the hand and ask you to go with them. I remember in the crowd of people on the street I once saw a little girl not more than six years old, all in rags, filthy, barefooted, hollow-cheeked, and beaten: her body was covered with bruises that could be seen through her rags. She walked as though unconscious of herself, without hurrying, going nowhere, wandering, God knows why, in the crowd; perhaps she was hungry. No one paid any attention to her. I turned around and gave her a half-shilling. She took the silver coin and then wildly, with frightened astonishment, looked into my eyes and suddenly took to her heels as fast as her legs could go, as if afraid that I would take the money from her."[8]

He paused, shuddering at the memory. "The British, they are so proud of their Crystal Palace. These writers, these Russians, so-called Russians." He again slapped the newspaper with his hand, "They think the Crystal Palace a perfect symbol of the world as it should be, as it will be. When I was there, I saw only a temple to Baal, England's true god, money."

"I have heard it is very impressive," Mikhail shot out without looking up.

"Oh, yes, it is striking. You feel a terrible force that has united all these people here, who come from all over the world, into a single herd. You become aware of a gigantic idea; you feel that here something has already been achieved, that here there is victory and triumph. You even begin to be afraid of something. 'Hasn't the ideal in fact been achieved here?' you think. It is a biblical scene, something about Babylon, a kind of prophecy from the Apocalypse fulfilled before your very eyes. It's the Bronze Horseman, coming to life to chase poor clerks through the streets of Petersburg. You feel that it would require a great deal of eternal spiritual resistance and denial not to succumb, not to surrender to the impression, not to bow down to fact, and not to idolize Baal, that is, not to accept what is as your ideal."[9]

Apollinaria sat quietly. No use trying to talk now, not with Fyodor like this. Better to let him get it all out, exhaust himself, and settle.

"Freedom! They talk of the freedom of the West. I got a taste of Western freedom. In Paris, I was followed. In London, I visited Herzen and met Bakunin, and so my luggage was searched before I left."[10]

He took a deep breath, sank into the chair next to Apollinaria and took her hand. "Forgive me, forgive me. These journals . . ." He took another breath, and a back door opened.

~

"Fyodor is off with another rant, I hear. As does all Petersburg." One of the editors of *Time*, Nikolay Strakhov, emerged from another room holding a piece of paper. He bowed slightly to Apollinaria and walked to Mikhail's desk.

"When the lion roars . . ." Fyodor was nearly angry.

"Of course you object to Western ideas, Fyodor, for you object to logic."

Fyodor waved him away with a hand. "No, no. I do not object to Europe or the West. I object to anyone who thinks that the West is our Savior from all evils. We have had this conversation before, Nikolay. Up one hill of Italy and down another, from Milano to Bologna to Florence, and back. Always the same."

"He will not listen to simple logic," Strakhov persisted, pleading with Apollinaria, showing a flash of anger himself. "I often lead our reasoning to the conclusion that, in the simplest fashion, can be expressed as: 'but really, it is impossible that two plus two does not equal four.'[11] But he will not listen. It is as if logic means nothing."

"I can say two plus two equals five if I choose," Fyodor answered.[12]

Strakhov spread his hands with an air of triumph.

"You completely misunderstand, Strakhov. Completely. Here is a radical, a nihilist let us say, who says, 'two plus two equals five.' You answer with logic and mathematics. But that is no answer at all to him because he does not believe that two plus two equals five, not really. If they claim to believe it, it must be because they are affirming something else. When these underground men protest against mathematical arguments that are put to him, they are standing up for one of the greatest values in the world, human freedom, and they are protesting the scientific denial of human freedom that is so prevalent today. Strakhov, when we are dealing with radicals, logical refutations are completely insufficient."

Strakhov grunted. "Human beings are beasts and nothing else. Irrational beasts. They say, 'two plus two equals five' because they are perverse."

"Now you are talking like an Augustinian," Fyodor shouted. "A rusty old Westerner if there ever was one! I do not agree. With my whole soul, I do not agree. It is a lie, a slander against mankind."

"Surely you have not turned liberal, Fyodor! You do not believe those Enlightenment fables about the inherent goodness of man. How can you? You've been among the reprobates."

Fyodor stiffened in his chair and looked coiled to spring. He relaxed himself and said heatedly, "Do not call them that. I despise liberalism. But I still say that human beings retain some semblance of good. I know that it is true of Russians. Christ still lives in us, still is with us, even now, and He does not abandon us."

"You are impossible. Impossible!"

"And you, my friend," Fyodor said, "have a defect of character that I hate, despise, and will persecute until my dying day."[13]

"Come, come. Let us be friends. There are enemies enough to fight out there," Mikhail murmured from the desk.

"Then I shall go find them," Strakhov said, stamping to the door, grabbing his coat, and slamming the door behind.

Mikhail gazed at his brother and shook his head.

≈

"Mikhail," Apollinaria said quietly, "may Fyodor and I have a moment alone?"

Mikhail gathered his papers and stepped into the back room, closing the door quietly behind him without looking back.

Fyodor looked at her intently and took her hand. "Dearest . . ."

"I have something to say. I am leaving." Fyodor gasped. "I am leaving for Europe."

"But why . . . when . . . ?"

Apollinaria could not look at him. He looked like a small boy, helpless, alone, searching for his lost mother.

"I am leaving soon, in the spring, but I hope that you will come to see me."

"In Europe?"

"In Paris. I will be in Paris by next summer. I would like you to meet me there. We would have time alone, time to see things."

"Marya . . ."

Apollinaria said nothing for a few moments then, under her breath, "If you wish to stay here with your sick wife . . ."

"What shall I say to her?"

"Cultured gentlemen lie. If you didn't want to lie, you shouldn't have found a mistress."

Fyodor winced. "I cannot be without you. I cannot." He held her hand tighter. "I do not want to lose you."

Darkness passed over Fyodor's eyes. He said, almost in a whisper, "I will make the arrangements. I will be in Paris by the summer."

COAL OF FIRE

I killed her, Maikov. I killed her, and in killing her I killed myself."

"Another house of the dead."

"Another Job, stripped naked. A sword cut through my breast and tore out my heart."

Maikov began to speak, trying to think of something soothing to say. Fyodor was falling into one of his self-flagellating moods, and he would not be comforted.

"Here I was running all over Europe with Suslova, and back at home . . . I can hardly think of it. At every instant, Marya was seeing death before her eyes. She was afflicted and became desperate. Her nerves were completely worn out. Her chest was very bad, and she was as thin as a rail. It was terrible! It was awful to see this!"[1]

"Yes, I remember. I was there, early in 1864. Don't you remember?"

Fyodor looked at him blankly.

"It was terrible to see how much worse Marya Dimitrievna looked: yellow, nothing but skin and bones, the very image of death. She was very, very happy to see me, but her coughing placed a limit on her talkativeness."[2]

"And I could do nothing. I did nothing. I killed her."

"I remember it differently. I remember that you would divert her with various trifles, little handbags, piggy-banks, etc., and she seemed very pleased with them. You were both ill, you know. You were a very sad picture: she with tuberculosis, and you with epilepsy."[3]

"Oh yes, I was ill. Ill for months at a time, and even when I recovered I was not entirely well. But my wife was dying, literally dying. All that April, until the last day—April 16, I will remember forever—every day at some moment we expected her to be going. Her sufferings were terrible and it worked on me horribly because . . . because . . ."[4]

"You did love her. I'm sure of that."

Fyodor stared at the light and sat silently for a few moments. "She loved me immeasurably, and I suppose I also loved her the same way. But, my friend, we were not happy together. Not happy. It was her strange, suspicious, unhealthy fantastic character that made us positively unhappy together. It was very strange. We were unhappy, but we could not cease loving each other. But that is not quite it either. It is stranger than that. We loved each other despite our unhappiness, and in some way the unhappier we were, the more we became attached to each other."[5]

"Like one of your novels." Maikov risked a small joke, hoping to break the melancholy of his friend's mood.

Fyodor smiled wanly. "Yes, very much. Very much." He sighed. "Unhappy as we were, I still believe with all my heart that she was the most honorable, the noblest, and the most magnanimous woman of all those I had ever known in my life."[6]

Maikov glanced at the door.

Fyodor relaxed and smiled. "Until I met Anna, of course. Until I met Anna."

≈

Apollinaria came to the door shaking like a leaf in high wind. She had been crying.

The clerk at the desk had pointed Dostoevsky to her room with a knowing smirk. *Damn the French! So arrogant!*

She stopped in shock when she saw him standing at her door, still holding his luggage. He had just come from the train. "Fyodor! What are you . . . ?" She wheeled quickly and returned to her room. Fyodor followed her.

"It's too late," she sobbed as she threw herself on her bed.

Fyodor stood stupidly, stunned. "Too . . . late?" He felt faint.

She recovered herself enough to say, "I was just sending a letter." She handed it to him.

Fyodor's hands were shaking. He threw his bag onto the bed, pulled off his gloves, and sat down trembling. As if floating through a dream, he tore the envelope open and unfolded the letter.

"You are coming too late. Only very recently I was dreaming of going to Italy with you, but everything has changed within a few days. You told me one day that I would never sur-render my heart easily. I have surrendered it within a week's time, at the first call, without a struggle, without assurance, almost without hope that I was being loved. Don't think that I am shaming you, but I want to tell you that you did not know me, nor did I know myself. Good-bye, dear!"[7]

The letter slipped from his hand as he rushed to the bed and lay down at her side. He took her hand, pressing it hard, convulsing. "I must know everything. Tell me everything, or I'll die." He knelt at the bedside, put his arms around her knees, and buried his face in the bedclothes, sobbing like a child. "Polina, oh Polina! I have lost you! I knew it! I have lost you!"

Both of them calmed, and Fyodor asked in a quiet voice, "Tell me everything. Tell me, no matter how painful it is."

She had met Salvador, a young and dashing Spaniard, soon after she arrived in Paris. They had fallen instantly and madly in love, and she had come completely under his power. They were inseparable, day and night, but now for several days he had been avoiding her. His excuses made her suspicious, and she finally discovered that they were no more than excuses. He was trying to escape the affair as quickly as possible.

"He will not answer my letters." She was no longer cry-ing. She was becoming hysterical and beginning to scream. "I am going to kill him. Look, Fyodor, look." She pointed to the corner of her room, where there was a pile of ashes in a small basin. She laughed. "I burned some of my notebooks and let-ters. I am going to kill him!" More mad laughter.

"No, no, my love. You have lost him, but I am here. He is

handsome, young, glib. He swept you off your feet. But you will never find a heart such as mine. I am here, and I still love you."

≈

She turned to Fyodor with a sadistic smile on her face. "You are right. I would not like to kill him . . . that is too easy. I would like to torture him for a very . . . long . . . time."

They had been sitting in the hotel room for hours. Apollinaria alternated between screaming frenzy and cold, calm hatred. Fyodor was not sure which was more frightening.

"You must simply forget it. He has betrayed you. He is a cad and a gigolo. You will do best simply to forget him."

"I mistook him. I thought he was in love with me. Now I see the truth. I have sullied myself, but it was only an accident. Salvador is a young man, and young men need mistresses. I happened to be available, so he took advantage of me, and why shouldn't he have done so?"

"Yes. Yes." Fyodor stroked her hand.

She straightened and her eyes flashed. She rose and walked resolutely around the room, showing some of her old confidence and strength. Her face brightened. "I have it." She rushed to the bedside table, opened a drawer, and drew out some paper, an envelope, and a small pile of francs. She sat down at the desk and scribbled a note, which she proudly showed to Dostoevsky.

"You are paying him for his 'services'?" Fyodor glanced at her face, which was glowing with triumph.

"You said it yourself. He is a gigolo. Why not treat him as

one?" Apollinaria looked as if she might begin to dance and sing an aria.

"I have lost you, I know," Fyodor said after she handed the letter to the bellboy. "I have lost you as a lover. But I am happy that I have met a human being such as you. I am happy to know that such human beings live in the world at all. I beg you, please remain my friend."

Suslova watched him carefully.

Fyodor continued, "I have some hope that we can someday return to the love we had before. But that is no matter. Whether I have reason for hope or not, there is no reason why we cannot follow our plans. We can still go to Italy together. We can live like brother and sister, like old friends, which I hope we are and will remain."[8]

≈

"Fyodor, I need you."

They were in Baden, in adjoining hotel rooms. Fyodor opened the door and peeked around.

"What can I do, my love?"

Apollinaria was lying in bed. As Fyodor walked toward her, she drew back the covers. She was naked. Fyodor stopped.

"Come closer, Fyodor, I need you. Come closer. Don't be afraid."

Fyodor was beside the bed now, trying not to look at her body, the body that he had once enjoyed and still longed for, before Salvador, before all this.

"Kneel down. I need you to hold my hand." Apollinaria

took his hand and clasped it to her breast. Fyodor reached to embrace her with his other hand, but she pushed him away.

Fyodor tried to pull away, but she held on. "Don't go. I need you." She held his hand and gazed into his face. She was almost laughing, more mad laughter.

Salvador was out of reach, but at least she could get some vicarious satisfaction out of torturing a willing substitute. She held the sword and gleefully ran it into Fyodor's heart, again and again and again, until she had torn it out by its roots.

"I visited Turgenev today." Fyodor was desperate. "He's living with his mistress and her husband. He gave me a manuscript . . . his latest book. He wants to publish it in *Time*."

Polina stared uncomprehendingly at him.

"I should be reading the manuscript . . . so I can give Mikhail . . ."

She pushed his hand away with such force that he nearly fell backward. She pulled the covers back over her. She was screaming. "Get out! Get out! You ruined me. You ruined me for any other man. No man will love me again. They will all be Salvador."

Fyodor fled from the room.

≈

Fyodor rushed into the room waving a wad of francs wildly in the air.

"10,000! I just won 10,000!"

Apollinaria looked up from the book she was reading with a questioning look.

"Roulette. I have been at the roulette table." He was so breathless that Apollinaria worried that he might fall into a fit. "I won, and I won a great deal of money. Look!"

They had been in Baden for two weeks.

He paced the room excitedly. "I have been watching the games, other players, for a week now, and I have figured it out. I deduced one conclusion which seems to me reliable—namely, that in the flow of fortuitous chances there is, if not a system, at all events a sort of order. This, of course, is a very strange thing. For instance, after a dozen middle figures there will always occur a dozen or so outer ones. Suppose the ball stopped twice at a dozen outer figures; it will then pass to a dozen of the first ones, and then, again, to a dozen of the middle ciphers, and fall upon them three or four times, and then revert to a dozen outers."

Apollinaria understood none of it but was afraid to interrupt.

"I have developed a system, and if I stick rigorously to my system, then happiness is in my grasp. Our grasp. We will not have to worry about money again."

"A system." Apollinaria's voice was heavy with skeptical sarcasm.

"This secret . . . I really know it. Oh, it's terribly stupid and simple. It's childish how simple it is. Anyone can figure it out, though it is harder to perform than to discern, I am sure."

Apollinaria knew that she could not continue reading until she had heard it all. She laid the book on her lap, waiting for him to go on.

"It consists in holding oneself in at every moment and not to get excited, no matter what the play. That's all. Just keeping oneself under control, refusing to let the excitement of winning take over. Then it's absolutely impossible to lose, and one is sure of winning."[9]

The laugh that Apollinaria tried to suppress came out as a snort. "You're going to control your excitement? You?"

"Laugh if you will," Fyodor was saying as he closed the door behind him. "I will soon return with a stack of francs twice the size. You shall see."

≈

Back in Petersburg, Marya was on her deathbed. When Fyodor returned home, he spent days sitting at her bedside, contemplating the sorrow and strange love of his marriage.

8

A SWORD IN THE BREAST

I killed her, but in her death I began to see what life is. I began to see what Christ means when He promises us eternal life. Christ commands us to love our neighbors, does He not?"

"It is the second great commandment."

"Yes, precisely. And yet, that is completely impossible. We cannot do it. The law of personality on earth binds us. The ego stands in the way. Instead of giving ourselves to others, we seek our own way and prefer ourselves to others. I know that this is true of my life. Did I think of Marya? Did I think of Mikhail and his load of work? No, I wandered Europe with a woman to whom I was not married, a woman who didn't even want me. My ego drove me, not Christ's commandments. But I daresay that you could say the same. Your life, too, is more about fulfilling your ego than it is about loving your neighbor."

Maikov nodded. "Guilty as charged."

"It's even worse today than ever before. We're in the epoch

of dissociation. All are dissociating themselves, isolating them-selves from everyone else, everyone wants to invent something of his own, something new and unheard of. Everybody sets aside all those things that used to be common to our thoughts and feelings and beings with his own thoughts and feelings. Everybody wants to begin from the beginning. We used to be united, but the links are broken, and everyone acts on his own accord and finds his only consolation in that. It makes the ego a heavier burden than ever."[1]

Maikov nodded.

"But look, in that there is a proof of immortality. It is strange, but there it is. Ego controls us in this life, and that can lead us to one of two conclusions. We can become pessimists and say that Christ's demands cannot and will not ever be met. But if that is true, then human life is completely senseless. Christ's commands are the way of true human life, and if they cannot be obeyed then there is no way to live humanly. We will never be truly human. The only alternative is that there must be an afterlife in which the ego is tamed and put in its proper place, in which we become finally capable of fulfilling Christ's com-mand. The clash between Christ's commands and our egoism is proof that there is another world coming when Christ's com-mands will be fulfilled. Either that, or we are all in hell already."

"And in the time being? What do we do while we are waiting for the afterlife when we can obey Christ's commandments?"

"Yes, yes. Of course, the commands of Christ present a transcendent ideal toward which we strive even now. Christ alone could love man as himself, but Christ is a perpetual eternal ideal to which we all strive and, according to the law of nature, should strive. Since the appearance of Christ as the ideal of man in the flesh, it has become as clear as day that the highest use a man can make of his personality—of the full development of his ego—is, as it were, to annihilate the ego, to give it totally and to everyone undividedly and unselfishly. All are responsible for all—that is the law of Christ. The law of the ego fuses with the law of humanism, and in this fusion both the ego and the 'all' mutually annihilate themselves one for the other, and at the same time each attains separately, and to the highest degree, their own individual development.[2]

"This is my social ideal, my 'socialism,' if you will. I often imagine a dialogue between the individual and society. The individual tells society, 'I give myself to you,' meaning that he offers his talents, powers, loves, and hates to the rest of society to serve others. He sacrifices for society. But then I imagine that society responds with, 'I give myself to you.' Society gives all its resources, powers, and gifts to serve the individual so that the individual can be fulfilled. Each gives itself wholly and totally to the other. And this is the imitation of Christ and at the same time the highest realization of man. It is the fusion of ego and self-sacrifice, of individual and society. The paradise of Christ is this fusion, and this is the goal toward which all history, whether of humanity in part or of each man separately, is only the development, struggle, and attainment."

"This is not the socialism of the radicals," Maikov observed.

"They want the Paradise of Christ without Christ Himself. They want that paradise now, here, and not in an afterlife. But, this is my point, it is only with an afterlife that we can attain this goal. Man on earth and in time will not achieve this fusion. Man on earth is only a creature in development, not finished but transitional. But if there is no afterlife, then there would be no one to enjoy the fulfillment of this process. It is completely senseless to attain such a great goal if, upon attaining it, everything is extinguished and disappears, that is, if man will no longer have life when he attains the goal. Consequently, there is a future life in paradise."[3]

"Senselessness or Christ, then? Christ or nothing?"

"Those are the only two choices. And those are the choices wherever we turn. Art, writing, politics, law, religion, all of it depends on knowing that there is an afterlife, a paradise of Christ. True religion is suffering, striving, and reaching for something that will only be fulfilled in a future life, a future paradise. Politics has to be carried out in the shadow of this same afterlife. We need to seek justice and harmony, but we need more deeply to understand that this will not be fulfilled here and now, never in this world. Attempting to bring the paradise to earth now can only result in tyranny and cruelty. Art, too, is suffering, a struggle to imagine and depict an ideal in word, stone, or paint that cannot be depicted in these material substances but always eludes them. Take away that struggle, and you take away humanity, everything that makes life worthwhile."

Fyodor stood and adopted a mocking pose as an orator. "All that, I learned at the side of Marya's deathbed. Suslova tore out my heart, and then Marya died. But I got a new heart in the bargain, a burning heart, a heart of flaming coal. And that gave me something to say. It gave me a message. It gave my tongue a song."

> With right hand wet with blood he thrust.
> And with his sword my breast he cleft,
> My quaking heart thereout he reft,
> And in the yawning of my breast
> A coal of living fire he pressed.

≈

Marya's death was only the beginning of sorrows. Less than three months after her death, Mikhail collapsed after an intense negotiation with government censors concerning an article in their newspaper. By July 9, he was dead.

Fyodor now had another reason to hate the censors. He was inconsolable. "How much I have lost with him! That man loved me more than anything in the world, even more than his wife and family, whom he adored."[4]

Mikhail's death robbed Fyodor of a brother, a close friend, and a collaborator in literary and political adventures. Mikhail was generous but never fawning, never flattering. He never tried to ingratiate himself to anyone. He could not hover over another person, dripping honeyed phrases and sweet words. He was an exceptionally decent man, and he conducted himself like the gentleman he truly was. He was highly educated, a gifted writer, an expert on European literatures, a poet, and a well-known translator.[5]

"How can I ever replace him?" Fyodor lamented as he considered Mikhail's gifts and career.

Mikhail's death left his brother hobbled by multiple responsibilities. He took on the burden of supporting Mikhail's widow and children, a financial burden he could ill afford given his own mounting pile of debt. His one source of income, the journal *Epoch*, had only been publishing for a few months and already owed a great deal of money to creditors who had helped the Dostoevskys launch their new enterprise.

"How can I go on without him?"

$$\approx$$

"It's necessary to take matters in hand with energy," Fyodor remarked to Wrangel one summer day. "I'm printing on three presses at the same time, without regard for my health and strength. I alone take on the work of chief editor and the reading of proofs. Alone I negotiate with authors and the censorship, correct articles, raise money, stay awake until six o'clock in the morning, sleep five hours a night, and I put the journal on its feet."

He rubbed his eyes with the heels of his hands and blinked. "I'm afraid it's already too late."[6]

His friend looked at him sympathetically.

Fyodor continued, "I realized as soon as Mikhail died that I had two roads: abandon the journal and turn it over to the creditors along with all the furniture and belongings, and take in the family. Then get to work, pursue my literary career, write novels, and provide for the needs of the widow and orphans. Another possibility: find the money to carry on the publication at whatever cost. At the time, I felt I had to continue, that it was the only way to honor my brother and to make a living." His eyes were still blurry, and he rubbed them again. "What a pity that I did not choose the first![7] Debts continue to pile up, every day new debts. It haunts me. I cannot sleep. It never leaves me alone. I would willingly return to prison camp if it would allow me to pay them off."

"Your family?"

"Oh, they've helped, they have been very generous. My uncle Kumanin willingly gave me a down payment on my inheritance, but it is not enough. I cannot tell you how overwhelming it all is. I owe 10,000 rubles in signed contracts, and 5,000 on my word; 3,000 has to be paid immediately, come what may. In addition, 2,000 are necessary in order to purchase the right to publish my works, a right now held as a guarantee on a loan, so that I can begin to edit them myself."[8]

Wrangel gave him a puzzled look. "You owe money so that you can purchase the right to your own work?"

"I know, my friend, it is desperate, desperate. But that is where I am. I was forced to it. It's Stellovsky."

"That shyster! Why would you make a deal with him?"

"I had no choice. He gave me a loan in July, last month, 3,000 rubles. I couldn't have continued a moment without it, and he knew he could take advantage. I must deliver a manuscript to him by November 1 of next year, or he gains the right to publish my works for nine years, without giving me a single kopek.[9] I can finish, I am sure, if I can just get time to think, to write and think, without creditors banging at my door every moment, without the business of *Epoch* distracting."

He would soon enough be relieved of the responsibility for editing the journal. All his work proved useless. He published two issues of the journal in 1865 but then had to give up.

"I need to get away," he sighed. "I am thinking of another trip to Europe. Apollinaria's sister lived here in Petersburg for a time, you know. I've visited her here. She's in Zurich studying now. I am sure she will make her mark. And if I go visit her, perhaps . . ."

Wrangel raised his eyebrows. "Again? Didn't you have enough of her last time?"

"I still love her. I love her very much, but already I wish not to love her. She does not deserve such a love."[10]

"Come, come, Fedya. Why torture yourself? Aren't there any women here in Petersburg to satisfy you?"

"Oh, there are women in Petersburg," Fyodor replied. Since Marya's death, he had hardly been pining, for either Marya or Apollinaria. He had spent several months courting Anna Korvin Krukovskaya, and despite their differences in age and temperament, Fyodor had proposed to her. Anna refused, wisely, but Fyodor's friendship with her and her family continued. "There are other women, but Apollinaria I have never forgotten. Perhaps I can see her again."

"I do not believe it will be a happy reunion."

≈

It was not a happy reunion. Dostoevsky met Suslova in Wiesbaden, but she had no interest in reviving their romance. "You've ruined me for all other men," she said bitterly.

Lonely and disappointed, and desperate for money as always, Dostoevsky turned to the roulette table. He lost, and lost again, and was soon destitute. He wrote Turgenev for funds and received some help. An appeal to Herzen was finally answered after much delay. Maikov sent money. Things were desperate.

His situation had gotten so bad that it was unbelievable. Early one morning, the hotel declared that they would no longer give him any meals, neither tea nor coffee. He went for an explanation, and the stout German owner explained that he did not deserve the meals and that he would send only tea. For several days, he ate nothing and drank only tea. All the staff treated him with an inexpressible, totally German contempt. *There is no greater crime for a German than to be without any money and not pay on time,*[11] he thought. *Damn them!*

Hunger was not the worst of it. "They hemmed him in and sometimes refused to give him a candle in the evening when some bit of the previous one was left over, even the smallest fragment. He felt that he was one of the pathetic losers from Gogol's stories.

How much like a Shkestakov![12]

≈

"I am distantly related to Katkov, editor of *The Russian Messenger*," Princess Shalikova told Dostoevsky one day over tea in Wiesbaden. "I might be able to convince him to publish your work."[13]

Dostoevsky nodded. He took a sip of tea and set the cup down, suppressing his initial reaction. *The Russian Messenger* was the most anti-radical journal in Petersburg. Katkov was a good fellow as such men go, but he could not publish in that magazine without betraying all his closest associates. For years, he and Mikhail had struggled to maintain a middle position between the pro-government intellectuals and the radicals, and he was not ready to tip to the government side now.

"In fact," the princess continued, "I have already talked with him. He's ready to offer you 125 rubles per folio if you will write a novel for *The Russian Messenger*."

"That's very generous. Thank you." *Principle or need? Damn it all. Why am I always the beggar? Why must I crawl?*

"I know you are working on something already."

"Excuse . . . Oh, yes. I am."

"Perhaps you could write to Katkov and explain what it is. I know he would be interested."

"Yes, I suppose."

"I'm very eager to hear, if you'd be willing to tell me."

Fyodor was again internally fuming about the situation. "Yes, of course. It is the psychological report of a crime. A young man, expelled from the university, living in the direst poverty, falling under the influence of the strange 'unfinished' ideas afloat, decides to break out of his disgusting position at one stroke. He has made up his mind to kill an old woman who lends money at interest. The old woman is stupid, stupid and ailing, greedy; she takes a high a rate of interest, is evil, and eats up other's lives. He thinks, 'She is good for nothing. Why should she live? It would be a good deed to kill her.' These questions befuddle the young man."

Fyodor squirmed in his chair and forced himself to keep his seat and behave in a semi-civilized manner, for the princess' sake if not for himself.

"So, he decides to kill her," the princess continued. "How horrible."

"It will be the most horrible scene I can imagine. Brutal, blunt, bloody, blood everywhere. But this student is convinced that he is doing it for a good purpose, in order to bring happiness to his mother living in the provinces, rescue his sister, finish his studies, go abroad, and then all his life will be upright, staunch, unbendable in fulfilling his 'human obligation to mankind.'"

"So he is a hypocrite."

"Oh, no, no. Not a hypocrite. Or, that is too easy. He is not a bad man. He is generous and good, in some circumstances at least. He is kind to a young girl, a prostitute, whom he meets at the Haymarket. Her name is Sonya, and this student— Raskolnikov is his name—he is kind and generous to Sonya and to her family."

Dostoevsky stopped and took a sip of tea. Some of it spilled out of the side of his mouth and dribbled into his beard. "Excuse me."

"Not at all. Go on."

Dostoevsky coughed for several moments. When he recovered, he went on. "He has done this horrible deed; he has tried to convince himself that it is noble. He is not a hypocrite, but he is human. He cannot live with what he has done. Heavenly truth, earthly law, take their toll, and he is finished by being forced to denounce himself. Forced because, even though he perishes in *katorga*, at least he will be reunited with the people; the feeling of isolation and separation from mankind, which he felt right after completing the crime, has tortured him. So the criminal himself decides to accept suffering in order to atone for his deed."[14]

"I cannot speak for Katkov, but I think it sounds fascinating. What do you call it?"

"*Crime and Punishment.*"

9

ARISE!

*C*rime and Punishment was the first novel I published with Katkov, in *The Russian Messenger*. It was a great success. I was at the top, at the top as I had not been since *Poor Folk*. And it was the beginning of a long association with Katkov, a long and fruitful one, I think."

"A long and protected one." Maikov smiled.

"True. When the radical papers were all being closed, Katkov was still running strong. The censors didn't have anything to worry about from him."

"But he had something to worry about from you."

"We had our differences. He had no sympathy for the radicals at all. No sense of what they really wanted, what their real motivations were."

Maikov cleared his throat. "Yet you were the one who called them devils."

"I did, I did. And I have nothing to regret. They were devils, quite thoroughly devilish. But they were young and needed to be guided, needed to have some chance to become men and women, some chance for freedom."

Fyodor looked into the fire. "1866. It was a remarkable year for me. It was the beginning of something new, a new epoch of my life. *The Russian Messenger*, Katkov, Germany . . ."

The silence begged to be filled. "And?"

"Stellovsky. I cannot forget how close I came to being enslaved to that man."

"It was a close call."

"I can never thank Milykov enough. You know, he visited me in September or October. The deadline was threatening, and I was frightened, distressed beyond all rest. It was Milykov who came to my rescue. He knew I couldn't write the novel in the time I had left, so he suggested that I retain a stenographer. That would speed up my pace. He found me a stenographer. He found me a savior."

There was a gentle knock at the door, and the door quietly opened.

"Just like that she came, Maikov, just like that." Fyodor rushed to the door and embraced Anna. "That is just how she looked then. I will never forget. October 5 . . ."

"October 4, my love."

"I will never forget. I opened the door, and there she stood on my front step. Anna Snitkina. A dove fluttering down from heaven. My savior."

~

Anna Gregoryevna Snitkina stood nervously at the door of

the great author's home on a chilly October morning in 1866. She straightened her hat and tried to tuck up a stray hair. She had been sent to serve as his stenographer. She was flattered that her stenography teacher considered her worthy of helping a legendary writer.

As she entered the apartment, she caught her breath. It reminded her of the house where Raskolnikov had lived. The study was dim and hushed, and she felt a kind of depression in that dimness and silence. Pasha, Dostoevsky's stepson, sat sulkily in the room, half dressed with hair disheveled and shirt open at the chest. Presently, Dostoevsky entered the room. His chestnut-colored hair, faintly tinged with red, was heavily pomaded and carefully smoothed. His face was pale and sick looking. He was dressed in a blue cotton jacket, rather worn, but with snow-white collar and cuffs.

He's much older than I expected, Anna thought.

As he spoke, he gradually became more animated and somehow younger.

His eyes struck Anna. *They aren't alike,* she mused. *One is dark brown, while the other has a pupil so dilated that I can't see the iris at all. The dissimilarity of his eyes gives his face an enigmatic expression.*[1]

"You must pardon me," he was saying. "I have just had an attack."

She looked at him questioningly but said nothing.

"Epilepsy, I suffer from epilepsy."

"I am sorry. I didn't know."

"Of course, of course." He adjusted his collar and ran a

hand over his hair. "It leaves me disoriented and confused for a time. I am afraid it makes it very difficult to concentrate on anything at all."

"I understand. Perhaps I should leave, come back tomorrow."

"No, no. You have come this far. Please sit down. May I get you some tea? Pasha!" he shouted. "Pasha, get . . . get . . . her some tea. I'm afraid I do not recall your name."

"Anna Snitkina."

"Anna. Anna. You come with a high recommendation. I hope you can help me. Thank you, Pasha. Here, my dear."

Dostoevsky tried to explain the situation but kept falling into silences. After some time, he looked at her sheepishly. "I believe I have wasted your time. You were right to begin with. I cannot work today, but perhaps you can come back in the evening?"

"Of course. Whatever will be useful."

When she returned in the evening, he spent most of the time recounting the story of his arrest and exile. Over the next few days, he was able to dictate a few pages of his novel, *The Gambler*, while novelist and stenographer got better acquainted.

≈

Fyodor Mikhailovich Dostoevsky ran headlong into the room. It was April 4, 1866. His friends looked up at him in alarm. He was terribly pale, looked in an awful fright, and he was shaking all over as if in a fever.

"The Tsar has been shot at," he shrieked, not greeting the others, in a voice breaking with emotion.

"Killed?" Maikov cried out in some sort of strange inhuman voice.

"No . . . he was saved . . . Fortunately . . . But shot at . . . shot at . . . shot at."

The others gave him a little something to quiet himself—though Maikov, too, was close to fainting—and all ran into the street.[2]

Petersburg was in turmoil. Under a bright blue early April sky, people were bustling here and there, and everyone was abuzz with the news. People who passed silently in the street on a normal day struck up conversations. A clump of men were talking excitedly at a street corner as Dostoevsky and his friends approached them.

"It was a student, I heard," one was saying.

"Dmitry something or other. Karazokov."

"No, Karakozov."

"But he missed. He missed?" Maikov interjected.

"That's right."

"Someone stopped him."

"Stopped him? Did anyone get shot?"

"I heard that someone bumped his arm, and the shot went off whizzing over the Tsar's head." His hand flew past the top of his head as he made a whistling sound.

"Osip Komissarov, that was the hero's name." This one had the cast of characters down pat.

"Count Osip, you mean," another said. They laughed.

"Tsarevich Osip. Alexander will adopt him, you'll see." They laughed again.

Dostoevsky and his friends wandered from clump to clump gaining what information they could. They visited the police station for news, but the police added little.

"This is worrisome," Maikov said as they returned to the apartment. "You know what will come. The officials will not take this lying down. They will shoot back, and they won't miss."

Dostoevsky nodded gloomily. "Katkov will be safer."

Maikov smirked. "One of the benefits of writing for a reactionary, I suppose."

≈

"I am a Slavophile, you know," Dostoevsky told Katkov one afternoon as the sunlight faded from the windows of the offices of *The Russian Messenger*.

Since the assassination attempt, many journals had been suppressed. Because of his opposition to radicals and support of the government, Katkov was safe from the government, and *The Russian Messenger* continued to publish and Katkov continued his fierce attacks on the radicals. Dostoevsky could not be silent.

"I believe Russia has a divine mission to the world. We need reform, but it needs to be reform that is consistent with our Russian institutions. I have longed believed that. We should not impose Western models of reform on Russia. That would be absurd. And I hate the violence as much as you do."

Katkov knew that there was a "but" coming.

"At the same time . . . I object to the way you speak of the radicals. All those high school pupils, those students, of whom I have seen so many, have become nihilists so purely, so unselfishly, in the name of honor, truth, and genuine usefulness!" he continued.

Katkov shifted in his chair. Talk like this made him profoundly uncomfortable.

"You know that they are helpless against these stupidities, and take them for perfection," Dostoevsky continued. "The innocents are convinced that nihilism gives them the most complete chance to exhibit their civic and social activity and freedom."[3]

"But they have become violent, Fyodor. One of them tried to kill the Tsar. They must be controlled."

"But where does that violence come from, I ask you. From their nihilism, you will say. I agree, but it is made all the worse by the police. Police breathing down the backs of students— that will not keep the students from being violent. It will make them worse."

Dostoevsky paused and looked out the window. He was thinking of prison and the lessons about freedom and slavery that had been burned into his heart by the experience.

"Even on your premises, suppressing free speech does not make sense. Do you know what the people are saying? They say that April 4th has proven mathematically the powerful, extraordinary, sacred union of the Tsar with the people. And such a union should allow certain government personalities to show more faith in the people and in society. Meanwhile, everybody awaits with fear more constraints on speech and thought.[4] It doesn't make any sense. If the Tsar is the head of a body, he should not be suspicious of his own body, should he?"

"What do you propose as an alternative?"

"Freedom, always freedom, Katkov. I favor free speech on principle, you know, but free speech is also the most useful political strategy that we have. How can nihilism be fought without freedom of speech? Suppose they, the nihilists, were given freedom of speech. They would make all Russia laugh by the *positive* explanation of their teachings.[5] If everyone could actually hear what they have to say, they would quickly lose their mystical authority. As it is, they seem to be sphinxes, enigmas, fountains of wisdom, secrecy, and this fascinates the inexperienced. Russian people are sensible. You know that, Katkov. That is your motto. Well, let us trust them to be sensible. Let the nihilists speak."

≈

During a pause in the dictation a week later, Anna spoke, "M. Dostoevsky. May I ask a question?"

"Yes, of course, my dear."

"Why are you so desperate to work on this novel? Is this the way you always work?"

"I should not make you carry my burdens." He sighed and sat down opposite Anna. "My brother died. Ever since then, I've been taking care of his family, of Emilya, his widow. And there's my other brother. He's a wonderful architect, a genius, but he drinks and drinks and needs my help constantly. I can't just leave him to himself. And there's Pasha."

Anna could not suppress a snort of disapproval. "I know, I know," Fyodor continued. "I realize that he's not a responsible young man. I have talked with him about that, again and again. But what am I to do? He's Marya's son, and I cannot simply abandon him."

"Aren't Mikhail's children already grown?"

Dostoevsky nodded.

Anna felt anger rising in her heart. "Yet they ask you, demand that you, take care of them?"

Dostoevsky shrugged slightly and slumped back. "I thought *Epoch* would support us all, but it didn't even before it closed forever. I cannot support everyone on the money I make from Katkov, welcome as that is. And there's another thing." Fyodor weighed the situation. How intimate should he be with this woman? He glanced at her eager face, now set sternly with indignation. *She is a great comfort to me, but she is so young, so young. Should I place on her such a burden? Would that be fair to her? Am I ready for a confidant? She already is a confidant,* he quickly reminded himself. *Whether I intended it or not, it's happened.*

"I made a very bad decision several years ago," he began slowly. "I was desperate for money, and the only editor willing to help me was Stellovsky. Have you heard of him?"

Anna shook her head.

"Pray you never have to deal with the man." Dostoevsky explained the contract with Stellovsky and the loss that Fyodor would incur if he failed to meet the deadline.

Anna's anger got the better of her. She stood quickly, and her pen and paper dropped to the ground. "That makes my blood boil!"[6] She was almost shouting. "How dare he? Make you buy back your own work! Who ever heard of such a thing? He is a villain, a covetous, greedy, conniving villain! I don't need to meet him, and I don't want to meet him. But if I do, I will give him a kick!"

Fyodor was afraid that she would kick over the side table. He put an arm gently around her shoulders. "Anna, Anna. I should not have told you. I had no right, no right at all to lay this on you. If you must be angry with someone, be angry with me! I am the fool who signed the contract."

Anna looked at Fyodor's face. She had only known him a short time, but already she considered him a wise, good, and yet unhappy man, though apparently abandoned by everyone. A feeling of deep pity and commiseration was born in her.[7]

She looked down, and when she looked again at Fyodor, his face was beaming with affection.

~

For Anna, pity was a degree toward love. Dostoevsky was also falling in love. He took to calling Anna his *golubchik*, "little dove," and came to rely on her more and more not only for the completion of his novel but as a companion, conversation partner, and advisor in life.

"I am at a crossroads," he told her one day. Creditors were bearing down, and he was considering whether to go back to the roulette tables of Western Europe or retreat into monastic exile in Jerusalem or Constantinople. "My other alternative is to marry again and seek joy and happiness in family life."

"By all means, marriage is the best of those choices."

Fyodor pressed on. "That is what I have concluded, but tell me your opinion. Should I marry a woman for her intelligence or for her kindness?"

"Intelligence. You are a writer, an intellectual. If you want kindness, get a nurse or a maid, not a wife."

Dostoevsky smiled. "I would incline rather toward kindness, so she'll take pity on me and love me."[8]

Anna was no fool. She saw where the conversation was heading, but she felt ambivalent about it. *He will certainly propose*, she thought, *but I really do not know whether I will accept or not. He is very pleasing, and it is exciting to be so close to the center of the literary work. Each day I leave here, full of ever fresh and original views of my favorite writer, and I live only in the expectation of the next day's meeting with him. What shall I do when he finishes his novel and no longer has need of a stenographer? At the same time, he frightens me with his irascibility and illness.*[9] *Could I live with that?*

Dostoevsky and Anna were working furiously to meet Stellovsky's deadline. With Anna's help, Dostoevsky's story was flowing smoothly now, and both were sure that the manuscript would be completed. Anna, practical and rightly cynical about the publisher, worried that Stellovsky would find some way to refuse the manuscript at the last minute. She contacted a lawyer, who suggested that they notarize the manuscript or register it with the police before submitting it to the publisher. It was wise advice. Dostoevsky finished dictating on October 29, and Anna brought him the written manuscript on October 30,

Dostoevsky's birthday. He made the final corrections and then tried to deliver the manuscript on November 1.

Stellovsky's manager told him that the publisher was on holiday, and he refused to accept the manuscript because Stellovsky had not authorized him to do so. It was too late in the day for a notary, so Dostoevsky went to the police station. The only officer who could register the manuscript was not in his office, and it was ten in the evening before he returned. Two hours before the deadline elapsed, Dostoevsky triumphantly left the police station with a receipt proving that he had met his contract.

Stellovsky's sword was no longer dangling over Fyodor's head. Anna, it was Anna who had saved him.

> Then in the desert I lay dead,
> And God called unto me and said:
> Arise!

10

AN ANGEL FROM HEAVEN

Come, my dove, sit down," Fyodor was saying. Anna wrapped her night robe around herself and sat quietly down on the arm of her husband's chair. "I was just telling Maikov about that day in 1866, that scramble from Stellovsky to notary to police station. I was frantic, hysterical." He stopped and chuckled. "I can laugh now. I was not laughing then."

"I can vouch for that," Anna said.

"Those few days marked the beginning of a new life for me. Free from Stellovsky, and then Anna's family invited me for dinner a few days later."

"At your suggestion," Anna said, touching his shoulder.

"I suppose I was shockingly forward. But it was necessary. I had to meet everyone."

"My mother was charmed."

"I was not trying to charm her."

"Yes, you were."

"Ahh, yes. But not only her. Anna, my dove, do you remember how I proposed to you?"

"How could I forget?"

"You must hear this, Maikov. Have I told you? Forgive me, I must say it again. Anna had come to the apartment to help me with finishing *Crime and Punishment*. I suppose I greeted her glowing with a heightened, fervid, almost ecstatic expression my face."[1]

"You told me that you had had a dream!"

"Yes, yes. A dream that I had found a diamond, a tiny one, but very sparkling and brilliant. I had found it among my papers . . ."

"'My dreams are always prophetic,' that's what you said."

"Did you know you were the diamond?"

"Of course, my dear. It was transparent."

"Then I told you the plan of my new novel. The novel's hero was an aging writer, sick with an incurable disease, gloomy, suspicious, a man with a tender heart tormented by his failure to embody his own ideals for his life. He meets a young woman who is gentle, wise, kind, bubbling with life and possessed of great tact in personal relationships. The writer falls in love, but he is again tormented by the sacrifice he is demanding of the young woman. What could this elderly, sick, debt-ridden man give a young, alive, exuberant girl? Could such a girl love such a man? Do you remember what you answered?"

Anna's answer was immediate: "'Why should this be impossible? Where is the sacrifice on her part, anyway? If she really loves him, she'll be happy, too, and she'll never have to regret anything.' That's what I said. Then you proposed."

"Yes, I tore off the fiction—a very thin veil, mind you—I

tore off the veil and asked you what you would answer if I were the author and you the young girl. I watched you carefully, very carefully, to see just how you would answer."

Anna looked affectionately at him and stroked his head. "I knew I could not hesitate or evade. You are so sensitive. If I wasn't straightforward with you, you would see right through me, and you would be devastated. I had to tell the truth."

"Do you remember what you said? Do you remember even now, my love?"

"I do. I remember as if it were yesterday. I remember it because it is the same answer I would give today, tomorrow, always."

"Tell me again, my love. Tell me and Maikov."

Anna looked steadily at Fyodor's face, aglow with the same excitement he had shown on that November day so many years before.

"I said I would love you and will love you all my life."[2]

≈

"Have you been crying, my dove?"

Anna had been sitting by the window watching the street for her husband's return.

"I have a pain on my inside. I'm not well. I think I have a temperature."

Fyodor took her hand and laid his dry cheek on her forehead. "I hope you are not getting sick. I shouldn't have taken you for that walk last evening. You have caught cold, and it's my fault."

He still loves me, Anna thought. *He is always so upset when anything is wrong with me.*

An hour before, Fyodor had gone out for cigarettes, sugar, and coffee, and he had returned with pears and strawberries in a basket. Pears! Anna so loved pears.

During his absence, Anna opened a letter that she had found in Fyodor's writing table, a letter from Suslova. As she read, she felt cold all over and shivered and wept with emotion. She was afraid that the old inclination was going to revive once more and swamp his love for his new wife. Just to think of it made her heart stand still.[3]

"I must lie down," Anna said as she walked to the bedroom.

Moments later, Fyodor was in the room, candle in hand, to see if she was still crying.

"Are you jealous on my account?"

He suspects that I know about the letter, Anna thought. She said, "Yes I am. I am jealous of that Englishwoman we saw out on the terrace." She laughed gaily, though her heart was full of terrible melancholy.[4]

≈

Fyodor and Anna had been married only a few months. Dostoevsky was able to secure an advance from Katkov for his next novel, and this money allowed him to afford the wedding, which took place at the Ismailovsky Cathedral in February 1867. His second marriage got off as inauspiciously as the first. Dostoevsky drank more champagne at the reception than he was used to and fell into an epileptic fit. He gave out a horrible, inhuman scream—or more precisely, a howl—and he began to topple forward.[5] Anna eased him to the floor and stroked his head on her lap until the episode was over.

Dostoevsky's health was not Anna's only worry. Dostoevsky's relatives continued their selfish demands on his money and time, and his stepson, Pasha, tried again and again to manipulate the newlyweds into quarrels. Fyodor's prodigal generosity made life difficult for a new wife to manage. Dostoevsky had always done most of his writing at night and slept through the mornings. Once he was awake, relatives and friends would arrive for lunch, and other guests would come for dinner. Anna was often sent off with the younger guests to a separate room from her husband, who discussed politics and literary matters with his older literary friends. Anna would have been much happier at his side and would have had an easier time without what she called his "disorderly hospitality."

Anna concluded that they had to escape the situation or their marriage would be endangered. Katkov had given Dostoevsky another 1,000 rubles as an advance, enough to take an extended trip to Europe. But relatives soon found out about Dostoevsky's money, and they came in with their demands. When the requests were added up, they exceeded the money that Dostoevsky had on hand. Anna was determined to leave, convinced that only a break from the family could save their love, their happiness.[6]

"I could pawn my dowry, my piano, my tables."

"I cannot ask such a sacrifice of you, my dove."

"It is a sacrifice. I am extremely fond of my piano, my charming little tables and whatnots, all my lovely things so newly acquired. But I will pawn them if it means we can leave Petersburg."[7]

She was able to raise enough money for the couple to leave for Germany on April 12, 1867.

≈

"I hate the Germans. The French are insufferable, but at least they are slightly human. These Germans run like clocks, tick-tock, tick-tock. It's like living in a machine."

"The hotel staff is pleasant, and I rather like their effi-ciency." She gestured toward the table, with its crisp cloth and neatly arranged ivory-white cups and saucers. Veal cutlets and roasted chicken steamed on their plates. "Even you have said you like our waiter—remember, 'The Diplomat.'"

"Pleasant if you like living in a machine. That's what this hotel is, a machine for living, and all the staff is just so many cogs. It will drive me mad."

Fyodor set down his knife. "What is this? How can they pass this off as butter? It is execrable."[8]

They sat at an outdoor table at the cheap Dresden restau-rant that Maikov had recommended.

He threw down his napkin and sighed. "I need Russia, need it for my writing, and how badly I need it! It's just like a fish being out of water; you lose your strength and means. The Germans upset my nerves, and the life of our Russian upper stratum and its faith in Europe and civilization do too!"[9]

Fyodor ordered an ice.

A uniformed Hussar passed on the street, staring straight ahead and walking, though off-duty, with a martial gait.

"Hussars everywhere! It's worse than the Russian police. Germany is a military camp from one end to another. Orderly, clean, without the least bit of freedom. I had more freedom in Siberia! What does the damned king of Saxony need with his forty thousand men? What is the use of that?!"

"I don't see why he shouldn't have them, if he can afford them." Anna cared nothing about Saxony or Hussars, but she was not going to listen to uninterrupted ranting all evening.

"If you are so stupid, then you had better hold your tongue."[10]

Anna recoiled as if she had been slapped but said nothing.

Fyodor sat back, exhausted.

This is going to be another unpleasant evening, Anna thought bitterly.

〜

Fyodor stopped at an arcade, picked up a rifle, and squinted down the barrel.

"You'll never hit anything."

Annoyed, Fyodor paid for a few shots. His first shot hit the bull's eye, and he turned triumphantly. "Well?"

He shot again, and again, and each time hit the bull's eye. "Well? Well?"

"A wife is the natural enemy of her husband," he insisted as they walked on.[11]

≈

Fyodor and Anna were lost. In good German fashion, the man they had consulted for directions sent them off to who knows where.

"Why don't you keep track of where we are going? How did you let us get lost?" Fyodor fumed. He was shouting.

"Is it my fault that we're lost? How should I know my way around?"

Anna was shouting too.

≈

Anna was crying again.

"You're nervy on account of the lonely life we live here," Fyodor was saying. "And you deplore ever having married me. You would like to leave me, wouldn't you?"[12]

Nothing Anna said could persuade him.

What does it all mean, this perpetual quarrelling between us? she wondered. *I contradict him only to have something to say, and then we quarrel and quarrel. Will it ever end? I will end it. I will say nothing more all day.* They sat in silence for a few moments, and then she looked up at Fyodor. He was staring at her with a look of pure anguish on his face, and her heart melted. *I simply can't be cross with him. I show a severe face, but I've only to look at him for all my wrath to melt away.*[13]

≈

"What were you saying to that handsome young German?"

Anna roared at the thought of it. "I have never seen that

young man in my life. It was nothing, nothing at all. Why should you be jealous?"

Fyodor hung his head. "It was stupid of me to be jealous, I admit. Still, my suspicions are always there. I am sure someone will steal you from me."[14]

⁓

Anna woke up shivering. She had spent the previous evening reading about the Battle of Waterloo in *Les Miserables* and she dreamed she was on the battlefield. Wounded soldiers, blood flowing—it was horrible. She was with Fyodor, but he wouldn't protect her. She was shivering with cold, but he wouldn't give her any covering. She shivered and shivered through the night.[15]

⁓

Anna could not stop laughing. They had been quarreling about Russia and Russians and every little thing. Fyodor had called her stupid, which amused her very much. Fyodor glared.

The waiter brought the change and looked curiously at Anna. As he walked away, she called after him. "Is this the right change? Do these five pennies equal half a silver groschen?"

The waiter was offended, grabbed all the change, and stalked off.

Fyodor sat back in astonishment. Anna was still laughing, and Fyodor joined in. Anna simply shook with laughter, and even the waiter began laughing.

"It's because you are so easy to take in," Fyodor said. "The rogue is laughing because you are so easy to gull."[16]

Anna gazed at her husband. *This is the secret,* she thought. *I don't want to be cross with Fyodor, and I really cannot be. I will always begin to laugh and turn every quarrel into a joke. That is the secret.*[17]

≈

"That hat suits you well."

Fyodor had just come in from shopping, carrying cigars, cigarettes, some fruit, and some cheese. Anna was amazed at his ability to handle domestic tasks like shopping. He was wearing a brown hat.

Fyodor was as flattered as could be. "Do you really think so? Hmm. I guess it does suit me very well. Yes, it does."

What a child he is, Anna thought. *What a dear, sweet child.*[18]

≈

"Don't kill anyone," Fyodor ordered.

They were back at the arcade, and it was Anna's turn. "Here, hold it like this."

Anna took the rifle nervously, aimed, and managed to hit the Turk. She turned triumphantly to Fyodor and exclaimed, "Na!"

She immediately turned and tried again. "You have to load it, my love." She turned and glared, and Fyodor stuck out his tongue.

Her second try went awry.

"Don't kill anyone!"

They were both laughing.[19]

≈

Fyodor was away, gambling in Hambourg, and Anna was in a bleak mood. He promised to return in four days, but the days dragged on and on, and still no Fyodor. He wrote, promising to come, but he was not on the train. He wrote again and still did not come. He wrote to tell her he had lost everything, then he wrote again for more money.

Anna was angry, but more lonely than angry. Without Fyodor, something was missing. Without him, joy ceased to be joy. Even the most beautiful things made her sad because she had no Fyodor to share them with.

He is such a dear, sweet husband. When he is not in one of his moods.

Another letter from Suslova lay on Fyodor's writing table. Anna took a knife and cautiously opened the envelope. *What a stupid, clumsy letter,* she thought as she read. *It says little for the understanding of the writer. I am quite sure she is furious about Fyodor's marriage, and her annoyance is easy to see from the tone of her letter.*

She read it twice, folded it, and put it back into the envelope. At the mirror, she saw that her face was covered with little red spots from the excitement.

From Fyodor's desk, she brought out a box and opened it. It was full of his letters. Many she had read before and had been struck by the beauty of his writing.

She settled back on the sofa and began to read.

≈

"Don't you see, Fyodor? The opera was about us. It was about our quarrel. Here, let's try."

Anna paused, then began to sing softly, "Fyodor, my darling, my sweetheart, forgive me, I beg you."

Chuckling, Fyodor began to sing back, "No, no no, not for anything!"

"I beg you."

"No, no no! Not for anything in the world." Fyodor's voice had risen dramatically.

Their quarrel ended, and by means of opera they buried the hatchet.[20]

≈

"Fyodor, for heaven's sake, get down!" Anna looked frantically down the hallway. "Fyodor! I think I hear footsteps. The guard is coming. Oh, we'll be removed! For heaven's sake, get down!"

Fyodor stepped off the chair.

"Thank you! Oh, thank you. What are you doing?!"

He pushed the chair closer to the wall and stood back up on it and leaned toward the painting. "They'll fine us. They will remove us and fine us! O, do please come back down."

Fyodor was staring intently at Hans Holbein the Younger's painting of the corpse of Jesus, which hung in a gallery at the Basel Museum. He seemed not to notice Anna's instructions.

"It is like nothing I have seen in Russia," he was saying. "Nothing at all like the flat, golden, Russian icons of

Christ. Holbein combines the realism, the humanism of the Renaissance, with the powerful religious passion of the Reformation. It is remarkable, don't you think?"

"It horrifies me."

"Look! The whole form is emaciated, the ribs and bones plain to see, hands and feet riddled with wounds, all blue and swollen, like a corpse on the point of decomposition. The face, too, is fearfully agonized, the eyes half open still, but with no expression in them, and giving no idea of seeing. Nose, mouth, and chin are all blue; the whole thing bears such a strong resemblance to a real dead body."[21]

"I am sure I hear a guard. Will you *please* get off that chair?"

～

"The Germans know how to do it," Turgenev said after gulping a fourth glass of vodka. "They are smart, scientific, the wave of the future. We ought to crawl before the Germans."

Dostoevsky was in Turgenev's home in Baden and was horrified by Turgenev's hatred for Russia and by his attachment to Western Europe.

"But why should Russia follow another nation's path? Shouldn't we follow our own? Should we establish some independence from Europe?"

"All attempts at Russianness and independence are swinishness and stupidity. It only shows how backward we are."

Dostoevsky restrained himself with an effort. "Ivan, you should purchase a telescope."

Turgenev gave him a puzzled look.

"You are a long way from Russia, and you can't make us out very clearly from here. With a telescope, you could make us out better."

Turgenev exploded and went into a rant. Dostoevsky interrupted, "What has Germany accomplished?"

"What has Germany accomplished?" Turgenev turned pale. "What has Germany accomplished? In talking like that, you offend me personally. You should know that I have settled here permanently, that I consider myself a German, not a Russian, and I'm proud of it."

Astonished at this declaration, Dostoevsky apologized. "I did not mean to offend."[22]

"And who are you? You, a person who, as a consequence of morbid seizures and other causes, is not in full control of his own rational capacities; and this opinion of mine is shared by many others."[23]

Dostoevsky controlled himself as he rose and took his hat and coat. "I did not mean to offend," he repeated before hastily leaving.

~

Dostoevsky read while Anna sat on the sofa with her back to him, like a child turning her back on her papa.[24]

She put down her book, stretched, and yawned. She touched his shoulder, and he pulled back his book to let her lay her head on his lap. "Tell me a story, Fyodor."

It had been a good day. Fyodor had been bright and lively

and happy all day. He put the book on the table. "Have you heard the story of Vert-Vert?"

Anna shook her head.

"Vert-Vert was a canary in a convent that the nuns taught to pray and sing holy songs. Vert-Vert became famous far and wide, and the nuns of a neighboring convent begged the loan of him for a few weeks, which, after much hesitation, was granted. It was called for by a carrier's van that plied between the two neighborhoods. On the way, Vert-Vert picked up all sorts of bad words and expressions from the carrier, and when all the nuns had gathered round him in the convent to listen to his songs and prayers, he bespattered them with oaths and made them nearly sink into the floor. They thought their rival nuns had done this on purpose and did their utmost to do the bird some injury. Finally, they brought it to the bishop, and when the bishop saw that he truly was spoiled, he turned him out."

Anna smiled and closed her eyes. Fyodor stroked her head.

"I love you, Fyodoritschka."

~

"Holbein is a painter of the first rank."

Dostoevsky climbed down from the chair and stepped back to examine the painting at a greater distance. Anna took his arm just as a guard stepped into the gallery. The guard looked suspiciously at the couple, frowned, and then moved through to the next gallery. Anna could not help but laugh.

"That painting made a deep impression on me," Fyodor said that evening at dinner. "It is a real Christ, a flesh and blood

Christ. That painting has helped me with the novel I am writing. All the thoroughly beautiful men of literature—Don Quixote, Pickwick, Jean Valjean—they all are like that Christ, vulnerable, beautiful in their weakness, and I am writing a book about just such a beautiful man. That painting will be a central symbol in my book."

Fyodor stopped and took a bite of veal and a swallow of wine. "So far as I can tell, it seems that at the present moment in our art, the genre of painting regards Pickwick as something of an ideal, and as far as I can gather from conversations with certain artists, they fear the ideal like some kind of unclean spirit. This is a noble fear, but it is prejudicial and unjust. Our artists need a bit more boldness, a bit more independence of thought, and perhaps a bit more education. 'One must portray reality as it is,' they say. Well, I say that the ideal is also reality and is just as legitimate as reality. And ideals are essential to art, essential to being human."[25]

"You are quixotic to the marrow of your bones."

Fyodor laughed. "Exactly the right word, you know. It was Heine, wasn't it, who told about how, when reading *Don Quixote* as a child, he burst into tears when the hero was overcome by the wretched realist, the barber Samson Carrasco. I agree with Heine. There is nothing deeper and more powerful in the whole world than this piece of fiction. It is still the final and greatest expression of human thought, the most bitter irony that a human is capable of expressing. If the world ended and people were asked, 'Did you understand anything from life on earth?' a person could hand over *Don Quixote* and say, 'Here is my conclusion about life.'"

Fyodor was enjoying himself, enjoying the chance to talk and talk.

"You would be astride Rocinante if you could," Anna said. "Trying to impress the neighbor girls by making up romantic names for them," she added.

"I am not another Quixote. But perhaps I can create one."

Anna had listened to her husband's summary of the book many times. The "beautiful man" was Prince Myushkin. As the novel begins, Myushkin is returning to Petersburg from convalescence in a Swiss sanitarium. He is innocent, joyful, a holy fool. He quickly wins people's confidence because he is completely without ego. He sympathizes deeply with everyone he meets, and he embodies Christ in his life.

"But I do not want only to present a Christlike man," Dostoevsky told her. "I want to put my ideas and ideals to the test. I want to subject even my most cherished beliefs and ideals to rigorous and even brutal criticism. Myushkin embodies much of what I believe is ideal about human life. He is the most obvious Christ figure in all of my novels. Yet he finally makes a mess of things, precisely because he lacks the capacity to decide to pursue one love over another. Because he loves all equally, he cannot act, and his inaction ends in sadness and tragedy. Christ is the ideal, but the ideal of Christ won't be realized here. Only in eternity, only then will we be like Christ."

≈

During their stay in Germany, Anna became pregnant, and she gave birth to their first child, Sonya, on March 5, 1868, while the Dostoevskys were still in Geneva. As so often happened at a key moment in his life, Dostoevsky fell into an epileptic fit on the night that Anna went into labor. After some sleep he recovered, but he was so nervous that Anna asked that he stay outside the room. As soon as he heard his daughter's first cries, he burst into the room to see her.

"Sonya is a healthy, robust, lovable, marvelous child, and I could spend practically half the day kissing her and can't tear myself away," he told Anna a few weeks later. "She is only a month old, and she already absolutely has my expression, my physiognomy even to the wrinkles on my forehead—when she is lying down—it's exactly as if she were writing a novel!"[26]

Sonya was christened on May 4, Anna's mother and Maikov standing in as godparents. Anna, who had been seriously ill, was advised to walk with Sonya, but during the walk Sonya caught cold. Her lungs became inflamed, and on May 12, she died.

Dostoevsky sobbed and wept like a woman, standing in front of the body of his darling as it grew cold and covering her tiny white face and hands with burning kisses.

"Oh, Anna," he cried. "This tiny, three-months-old being, so pitiful, so miniscule—for me was already a person, a character. She began to recognize me, to love me, to smile when I approached. When I, with my ridiculous voice, sang to her, she liked to listen. She did not cry or wrinkle her face when I kissed her; she ceased to cry when I approached. And now they tell me, in consolation, that I will have other children. But where is Sonya? Where is that little individual for whom, I dare to say, I would have accepted crucifixion that she might live?"[27]

"Europe killed her," Anna said between sobs. "I am sure she would have lived if we had been home."

"Then we must go home. As soon as we can, we will go home."

≈

Fyodor had nothing left. Before returning to Petersburg, Fyodor made one last try at the roulette table. He gambled away his money rapidly and then placed a further bet using the money that Anna had set aside for the return trip to Russia.

"How vile I have been! Anya, my guardian angel! A great thing has been accomplished within me, a vile fantasy that has tormented me almost ten years has vanished. For ten years (or, rather since my brother's death, when I was crushed by debt), I kept dreaming of winning. I dreamed seriously, passionately. Now all that is finished. This was absolutely the last time! Will you believe, Anya, that my hands are untied now; I have been bound by gambling."[28]

Anna had heard such vows many times before, but this time was different. He never returned to gambling again. This disease, at least, had been cured.

≈

Fyodor climbed into bed early in the morning after a night's work. He put his arm around Anna, pulled her nearer, and kissed the back of her neck. She half woke up and smiled.

"Did you get your work finished?" She snuggled against his chest.

"Wery efficiently," he said. "It vas like de working of de clock. Tick-tock, tick-tock, the words came out. I vas a machine for writing, an efficient German machine. Germany is rubbing off on me, and soon I vill be as unfeeling and stolid as a rock."

Anna giggled.

"Forgive me. I was irritable this afternoon, angry at you and angry at the world. I don't know how we are going to continue to live. I worry about money all the time."

She turned her face to his and kissed his lips. "Something will turn up," she said, her eyes dancing.

He pulled her closer to kiss her, and she closed her eyes. "You are an exquisite creature, sent from heaven. You are a saint, devoid of sin, the darling of my heart. You come from paradise to bring me there." She knew none of it was true, but oh, how she loved to hear it!

"I have only one thing against you."

Anna turned to see if he was joking. He was.

"You lack experience. If you had an ounce of sense, you would never have married an old, slovenly, toothless sinner such as I am."

She lived for the small moments, late at night, when he came to bed after a night's work. They would talk together for ages, and he would say pretty things and joke and laugh. To Anna, that was the time they seemed nearest together, and it was the most precious of all the hours of the day.

His rages don't come from his heart, she thought. *They are all on the surface. Beneath, his heart is good, and it is mine, truly and forever mine. At first he was so dreadfully touchy, and now he positively eats out of my hand! He used to get into such dreadful rages and scream so at the people in the house that I used to tremble to think of what the future would be with such a husband.*[29]

He kissed her again and gently drew her closer, then closer still.

LET MY VOICE BE HEARD

Did you ever know Ogarev?" Fyodor asked Maikov.

Conversation had drifted back to politics. Anna yawned.

"Only by reputation. I knew enough to know that his wife was Herzen's mistress for years and years."

"You heard correctly. I knew him when I was in Europe in the late sixties and early seventies. Do you remember him?"

Anna nodded. "He was so kind."

Fyodor agreed. "But his politics were ridiculous, absurd. We became friends because he was one of the few cultivated men I got to know in Europe. He had read a book. You know, he got me into the Congress of the League of Peace and Freedom once. Bakunin was one of the speakers." The Congress was an international activist organization promoting social and political reform across Europe.

"Did you hear him?"

"I didn't need to. I had heard enough of his ideas. He

was like all the rest. They began with the fact that, in order to achieve peace on earth, the Christian faith has to be exterminated; large states destroyed and turned into small ones; all capital be done away with so that everything be in common, by order, and so on. All this without the slightest proof; all of this memorized twenty years ago, and that's how it has remained. And most importantly, everything has to be destroyed with fire and sword—when everything has been annihilated, then, in their opinion, there will be peace.[1] It is a religion, but it is a religion of violence, blood, horror, terror, and destruction. Redemption by destruction, that is their gospel."

Dostoevsky laughed mirthlessly. "I saw this, I saw it was absurd, but then absurdity was added to absurdity. The police are idiots. I was a dangerous Russian writer, so I had to be watched. The Petersburg police opened all my letters while I was in Europe, and since the Orthodox priest in Geneva worked for the secret police, the post office in Geneva delayed letters addressed to me, and this I knew full well. All the while, I was devoting my every ounce of energy to exorcizing the demons from Russia."[2]

"I believe you did."

Dostoevsky could not help but smile with self-contentment. "I hope so. I hope so. But I know what really turned the tide."

Maikov waited.

"It was Nechaevism. That was the ghost that frightened the radicalism from the radicals, the nihilism from the nihilists. It gave a little hope for a little while."

≈

"He is a comic character," Fyodor said.

"Comic? How can he be comic? He is a radical, a murderer."

"Still, he is absurd."

On a bright spring afternoon in 1873, Fyodor and Vladimir Solovyev sat at a sidewalk café on the Nevsky Prospekt, drinking afternoon tea and discussing Dostoevsky's latest novel, *Demons*, and the Russian political situation that had given rise to it. While the Dostoevskys were still in Europe, they had heard the awful reports that Sergey Nechaev, a student from the Petrovsky Agricultural Academy in Moscow, had murdered another student at the Academy. Nechaev became a folk hero with the radicals. He had created a history and persona for himself that mesmerized the simple. He claimed to have escaped from the Fortress of Saints Peter and Paul and pretended to be part of a worldwide revolutionary group. Nechaev had some connection with Bakunin, and anti-radical writers saw the murder as the logical result of revolutionary ideas.

Three Dostoevskys—Fyodor, Anna, and their second daughter, Lyubov, born in Dresden on September 14, 1869—had returned to Petersburg in 1871. It was not an easy return. While Dostoevsky had been away, Pasha had pawned a good bit of his library, leaving him without many of his beloved books. The creditors soon found that he was back, and they were just as soon knocking at his door. Dostoevsky responded with frustration and hysteria, but now he was not alone. When a widow, Frau Hinterlach, demanded immediate repayment for a loan made to Dostoevsky by her husband, Anna went to visit her in person. Anna reminded the widow that if she forced the issue, Dostoevsky would be taken to debtors' prison, where he would be supported at Frau Hinterlach's expense. Anna threatened to bring the matter to public attention by publishing an article about it in the press, and Frau Hinterlach backed down and accepted payments. From that time on, Anna served not only as Dostoevsky's wife and stenographer but also as his business manager.

A week after their return, Anna had another child, a son, Fyodor, known as Fedya, and without the physical problems of her earlier pregnancy and delivery. While the growing family settled in, Dostoevsky was quickly brought into a circle of associates and conversation partners that delighted and challenged him. Through his connection with Maikov, he came to know the Prince V. P. Meshchersky, a friend of the Tsarevich Alexander, and Konstantin Pobedonostsev, a cultured lawyer and translator who rose later to be an advisor to Alexander during his time as Tsar. Dostoevsky met with members of the faculty at the University of St. Petersburg through the husband of his niece, a professor at the university. The Dostoevsky home was a place of continual hospitality, which included dinner with the socialist N. V. Dailevsky. Dostoevsky received financial support from the Tsar himself—minimal, but from the Tsar!

Over the following years, he also became acquainted with the brothers Solovyev. Vsevolod was a novelist and journalist and a great admirer of Dostoevsky, whose novels helped him form his own religious beliefs. His brother, Vladimir, a mystic and devoted student of esoteric lore, had also been weaned from nihilism by reading Dostoevsky, and he and Fyodor struck up a correspondence and later a friendship. He became a frequent visitor in the Dostoevsky home after 1873, and their friendship grew even closer in the last decade of Dostoevsky's life. They shared a passion for Christ and a passionate opposition to egoism of every kind.

"The revolutionaries of the 1860s have given birth to the nihilistic religion of violence of today," Fyodor said. "They gave rise to Nechaevism. But behind them all are the romantics of the 1840s. They are the fathers, who have had sons and now have grandsons. Sowing wind, reaping the whirlwind."

"So, Peter Vekhovensky, Stepan's son, is the Nechaev of your novel?" Vladimir asked. Dostoevsky nodded.

"And you think he is comic? I find him unsettling."

"He's absurd. He convinces everyone that he is at the hub of a universal revolutionary movement, but in the end there are only a few provincial locals, whom he has charmed into listening to him. Absurdity can be highly destructive. You see, I am trying to depict the diverse and multifarious motives by which even the purest of hearts and the most innocent of people can be drawn into committing such a monstrous offense. That is the real horror: that in Russia one can commit the foulest and most villainous act without being in the least a villain![3] One can commit a foul act and be an absurd clown."

"Like the absurdity of Turgenev . . . I mean, Karmazinov." Solovyev flipped the pages of a book with his hand.

"It is transparent, isn't it?"

Solovyev laughed. "As glass. Did you mean to disguise it? Fyodor, you are too honest to wear masks."

"May it be so," Fyodor said. He finally had begun his public revenge for Turgenev's satires of him.

"I loved this passage about Karmazinov," Solovyev continued. "'A year before, I had read an article of his in a review, written with an immense affectation of naïve poetry, and psychology too. He described the wreck of some steamer on the English coast, of which he had been the witness, and how he had seen the drowning people saved, and the dead bodies brought ashore. All this rather long and verbose article was written solely with the object of self-display. One seemed to read between the lines: "Concentrate yourselves on me. Behold what I was like at those moments. What are the sea, the storm, the rocks, the splinters of wrecked ships to you? I have described all that sufficiently to you with my mighty pen. Why look at that drowned woman with the dead child in her dead arms? Look rather at me, see how I was unable to bear that sight and turned away from it. Here I stood with my back to it; here I was horrified and could not bring myself to look; I blinked my eyes—isn't that interesting?"'"[4]

Solovyev was laughing. "It could have come from Turgenev himself! It's not the first tear that identifies the sentimentalist. It's the second tear that he sheds when he considers the overwhelming sensitivity of his first tear. The Germans have coined a word for it—*kitsch!*"

"What a wonderful Teutonic ring that has. *Kitsch!* Yes, you get my point. The romantics can only see their own feelings;

they lack all interest in anything but their own experience. They could not have known, but they were sharpening the knives and preparing the ammunition. Start with *kitsch*, and you end with Nechaev!"

Solovyev flipped through the pages, chuckling here and there as he went. He set the book down on the table. "It is a handsome volume."

Since the 1840s, Dostoevsky had dreamed of self-publishing, and after discussing it with Anna, he decided to publish the book. Anna visited bookshops to learn about the book business, and, despite their financial straits, they were able to get enough money to purchase the necessary equipment and materials to print 3,500 copies. Their first run earned them 4,000 rubles.

"Pay Anna your compliments. It is her doing. Nearly everything is, you know. If there's success at all in my life, it's Anna's doing."

"And how are things with Meshchersky?"

Fyodor covered his face with his hands and moaned. "Don't ask. It is terrible. He refuses to let writers write. He will not let any voice be heard that he hasn't approved. He would have been among the Israelites asking the Lord to stop talking from Sinai. If he heard the whirlwind of God approaching, he would ask it to quiet down."

"Prince Full Stop up to his old tricks."

They had moved from afternoon tea to pre-dinner vodka. Fyodor rolled a cigarette and lit it, coughing.

"If I had an ounce of courage, I'd tell Prince Full Stop to stop his mouth. Fundamental reforms cannot be brought to a 'full stop,' as he wants. It would be inhuman, but that is not the only problem. Too much has happened. It has become impossible. Our latest battle had to do with university students. Prince Full Stop wrote some absurdity about the government keeping surveillance on university students. I struck the line and then wrote to him passionately expressing my views on the subject. I told him that his ideas were deeply opposed to my convictions and that his editorial filled my heart with indignation. Do you know what he answered?"

Solovyev shook his head.

"'I presume you are not of the opinion that the students should be *without* surveillance.' That is what he said, his exact words: 'I presume you are not of the opinion that the students should be *without* surveillance.'"[5]

Solovyev looked sadly at his friend. His brother had told him how all the other journals attacked Dostoevsky as a madman, a maniac, a renegade, a traitor who belonged in a home for the feeble-minded.[6] He pitied him almost as much as he admired him.

"It is not all sorrow. I have been getting to know a young woman, a proofreader, Varvara Timofeyeva, a lively, opinionated young woman. I thought she was another mindless radical, but the more I talk with her, the more I realize that the radicals have changed. Nechaev was the turning point. The radicals recoiled. For decades, radicals have mocked Christian Russia, proclaimed themselves to be above moral constraints, celebrated the glories of personal fulfillment and egoism, and insisted that the world was only matter and motion. Once, egoism was the cutting edge of radical thought. With Nechaev, it became clear that this was a dead-end, that radicalism of this sort could only end in a celebration of destruction and murder. It is a remarkable change."

"I have heard Prince Peter Kropotkin talk of the need for a 'morally developed individuality' as the foundation of every organization.[7] The radicals of ten years ago would not have been found dead saying such things."

"It is most hopeful. At one time, they were all attracted to Pisarev, who told them of the great utility of the natural sciences in making a 'thinking realist' out of men. They wished to live in the name of 'cultivated egoism,' rejecting all authority. And they learn that there are other things besides the natural sciences. They've learned that the anatomy of frogs by itself does not take us very far.[8]

"And this is not theory, their *narodnichestvo*, their populism. I hear every week of young men going out to villages as doctors, doctor's helpers, village scribes, even as agricultural laborers, blacksmiths, woodcutters. Girls pass teacher's examinations, learn midwifery or nursing, and go by the hundreds to the villages, devoting themselves to the poorest part of the population. These people go without any idea of social reconstruction in mind, or any thought of revolution. They simply want to teach the mass of the peasants to read, to instruct them in other things, to give them medical help, and in this way to aid in raising them from their darkness and misery and to learn at the same time what were *their* popular ideals of a better social life."[9]

"They are even friendly toward Christ. Christ's voice is at last being heard."

Dostoevsky sat forward. "That is true, but Christ does not seek friends. He seeks disciples. And for all their virtues, these are not disciples. They want peasant values without peasant religion, and as always they want their good deeds without Christ. If you were to give all these grand, contemporary teachers full scope to destroy the old society and build it anew, the result would be such obscurity, such chaos, something so crude, blind, and inhuman that the whole structure would collapse at the sound of humanity's curses before it could even be completed."

"They want to stop playing with the word *God*, and they think that you're old fashioned because you won't stop."

"Nechaevism scared them, but they don't realize that the only way out of Nechaevism is Christ. Once having rejected Christ, the human heart can go to amazing lengths. That's an axiom."[10]

12

SPAN LAND AND SEA

Dostoevsky was coughing uncontrollably. Maikov patted his back and gave him a glass of water. "Drink something. It'll sooth your throat."

Fyodor waved him off. "It's not my throat," he said between coughing spasms. "Emphysema" was all that he could get out.

"Bad Ems has not helped?" Maikov asked when Fyodor had stopped coughing. Bad Ems was a spa town in Germany that Dostoevsky had visited several times.

"Not at all. Or not much. I have been several times, and it was hell. On the train from Berlin, we sat like herrings in a barrel, but that is nothing compared to the regimen of the spa. All of Ems wakes up at six in the morning—it was ungodly, but I also woke up—and at six-thirty several thousand patients were crowded around the two springs. We sang a boring Lutheran hymn. I don't know anything more sickly and artificial, but there you are. I drank a glass of the water at seven, took a walk, got a second glass, then returned home for my coffee. I had epileptic fits, and I came to hate every building, every bush. I was so irritable early in the morning that I viewed everyone as a personal enemy. And I worried about the children all the time and missed Anna terribly, terribly. I dreamed about her every night."[1]

Fyodor coughed again. "At first it seemed that there was improvement. I had less dry coughing; breathing was easier. And there were some benefits. I had time to read Pushkin, which I did with uncommon delight. And I began to prepare new novels there. All was not lost in Bad Ems."[2]

Maikov sat back down and looked at his friend. "I read Job again too," Fyodor was saying. "It always puts me in a state of painful ecstasy. I leave off reading and walk around the room almost crying, and if it weren't for the vile notes of the translator, I would be happy. That book, it was one of the first to impress me in my life. I was still practically an infant when I read it. And it still moves me. Even now it moves me."[3]

"It is the human condition. Every human problem is there."

"Yes, yes. It's all there. But it's also my condition. I see my life when I read Job. Loss and sorrow. Children, children suffering, children taken—and why?"

He choked on the words and began coughing again. Maikov looked at him sadly.

"I was crushed by his death. I loved Alyosha in a special way," Fyodor said quietly. "And what racked me was the fact that he died because of me—he died of epilepsy, a disease I gave him." Fyodor's second son, Alyosha, had died at the age of three on May 16, 1878, after a twelve-hour epileptic attack.

"Anna lost her bearings, she cried and mourned so much that I could hardly recognize her. It was hell, living hell. Give me prison camp, but don't torture innocent children!"[4]

"It's the life of Job. But Job did get children back, more than before."

"Did he love them, though? I wonder. Could he love his children after that loss? That's the question that tortures me. All I can say is, he did; he did. I cannot understand how, but he did. He could still kiss the ground and bow before the Lord, even after that. He did not turn in his ticket."

Fyodor sighed deeply. "I would never have made it through without Solovyev. He called on us again and again, and then he insisted on taking me off to the monastery, to Optina Pustyn. I was only there for two days, but what days! It had a profound and lasting effect on me. I met with Father Ambrose three times.[5] He told me that every time I weep for Alyosha I should remember that my little son is with the angels, that he looks down from heaven and sees me, and rejoices at those tears."[6]

Fyodor paused to cough quietly.

"This is my aspiration, to write such a book, to write a book as big as the great book of Job, where everything human is included. Everything."

"*Karamazov*—another name for mankind?"

Fyodor smiled, flattered. "*Karamazov*, the last and greatest of my works. I will finish it, and *The Children*, and then I shall die."

≈

"Will it work, Fedya? I don't know."

Anna was busy at needlework while Fyodor bustled around the sitting room. Lyubov was reading in a corner of the room, young Fyodor rocking back and forth on his rocking horse.

"We have no regular income, only the trickle that comes in from your books and from our little publishing house. I know that you want to make a regular income, but will this work? If it proves to be a failure, it will put us in a hopeless position."

"Oh, but it will work, Anya. I know it will, and it will do more than work. It will extend my audience even further than it has ever been. I had a following in the literary world as a young man. I have regained that, but my readers are still the readers who buy and read literary periodicals. What if I wrote directly to the people? What if I wrote about all the things that occupy their minds? I believe I can speak to them, forcefully, simply, and that I can give them greater insight into the world, everything that is happening around us."

"What would you write about?"

"Oh, everything. Everything I hear or read about. Crimes and legal cases, spiritualism, Russia and the West, new books, new art exhibits, wars and rumors of war."

"Blood, fire, vapor of smoke!"

Fyodor laughed. "Abominations and desolations. I tell you, I believe that it will be a great success. No one has ever written to the people like this before. It is one of the things I was created to do, I am sure. I know the people, I have lived with the people, and I can speak to the people. They will listen to me, and I can help Russia become the people that she is destined to become."

"Russia's prophet?"

"Complete with prophetic beard," Fyodor said as he stroked his chin.

"Will you write about me?" Lyubov had stopped reading to listen to her parents.

"Don't interrupt. This is important."

Lyubov frowned, glared, and went back to reading.

Fyodor's face turned grave. "I believe I have a mission, especially to the young. I fear losing touch with the younger generation, breaking with it. They must be brought back to the Russian ideal. They are the future, and they must know what Russia is for, why she exists at all. If I do not tell them, who will?"

"I do not mock you, my love. I believe you, and believe in you, with my whole heart."

Fyodor's face softened, and he smiled. "And the best is this: the *Diary* will not take time and energy away from my novels, as all the other editing has. It will be preliminary to my novels. While preparing to write a long novel, I will immerse myself in the study of the details of contemporary life, especially the younger generation and the Russian family. The *Diary* will be my research notes for the rest of my novels."

He started coughing and could not stop. He leaned over the table and, shaking, poured himself a glass of water. Anna looked worriedly up from her work.

"Do you have the strength?"

When he stopped coughing, he answered. "It will be only once a month—sixteen pages—and it will be published at the end of the month, the very last day. Anya, I want to make sure that I can make enough money to set you up for the future, when I'm dead and you're left with the children."

"You will be writing with your own blood."

"So be it." Fyodor was deadly serious. "I don't write for pleasure. I have a mission, and I will write and write until I have fulfilled it or die."

Fyodor was right. It worked. Nothing in his highly successful career gave him fame like the *Diary of a Writer*, which he published virtually every month between 1873 and 1877. He wrote about children and juvenile criminals, visits to prisons, séances and spiritualism, trials, women, art and poetry and fiction. The *Diary* had the widest circulation of any periodical of its time, and it found its way into the hands of the Tsarevich Alexander. Young people flocked to the journal, and many came to consider Dostoevsky something of an oracle.

"I consider my literary position almost phenomenal," he explained to Anna some months later. "How has a person who writes at the same time against European principles, who has compromised himself forever with *Demons*, that is, with reaction and obscurantism, how is it that this person, without the help of all their Europeanizing journals, newspapers, critics, has nonetheless been recognized by our young people, those very same young nihilists who have lost their moorings and so on? They all say they await a sincere and sympathetic word from me *alone* and consider me alone as a guiding writer. If the rest of the conservatives didn't know that, they would eat me alive, like dogs, but they're afraid and watching to see what happens next."[7]

"Consulted by nihilists in the afternoon, dinner with the royal family in the evening," Anna laughed. Though still under official police surveillance as an ex-convict, Dostoevsky had been invited to dinner by Grand Duke Sergey so that Dostoevsky could broaden the minds, especially of the younger members of the court.

"Altogether phenomenal," Fyodor said again.

Anna was right too. He did not have the strength. After two years, sick and weakened by the grinding schedule of writing to which he committed himself, Dostoevsky decided to stop publishing the *Diary*. But there was another reason. "I have a novel in my head and in my heart, and it's beginning to be written." He found that he could not combine writing the diary with writing a novel. One had to go, and he believed that his mission was bound up with the novel, the novel that would be as big as the book of Job.

⁓

"We were in the same room, Tolstoy and I. Count Tolstoy was disguised, and Strakhov hustled him away so that he would not have to meet anyone. At least he could have told me so that I could take a look at him. At least I could have seen him with my own eyes."

Fyodor was sitting at a table in a dim Petersburg tavern, sharing drinks with Solovyev. "I didn't meet him that night either. I wish I had known he was attending my lecture."

"It is no matter. You would not have said anything different. The lectures were an event, even without the presence of Count Leo Tolstoy."

Solovyev held a small glass to Dostoevsky, then threw it down his throat.

"I was especially struck by what you were saying about Catholicism."

"I really did hear that from a Jesuit. 'Of course'—he said—'no one at present believes in the greater part of Christian dogma. But we all agree that we cannot have a civilized society without strong authority and a firmly organized hierarchy. Only the Catholic Church possesses such an authority and such a hierarchy.' In the name of enlightenment—yes, that is what he was saying—in the name of enlightenment and civilization, everyone who values the interests of mankind must side with the Catholic Church. Every enlightened man must be a Catholic."[8]

Dostoevsky snorted. "That is a crucial part of my novel. It is all about the abandonment of Christ, abandonment by atheists and socialists, but just as much by Catholics. In the end, they are the same. They abandoned Christ when they abandoned freedom.

"It is the crucial scene in the novel," he continued. "A contemporary negator, one of the most ardent, comes right out and declares himself in favor of what the devil advocates, and asserts that this is truer for the people's happiness than is Christ. To our Russian socialism, which is so stupid, but also dangerous because the younger generation is with it, the lesson is very forceful—one's daily bread, the Tower of Babel, the future reign of socialism, and the complete enslavement of freedom of conscience—that is the ultimate goal of this desperate denier and atheist!"

"The temptations of Christ," added Soloyvev.

"Yes, exactly, exactly as you said in your lectures," Fyodor said. "But it is not only this atheist and nihilist. He has written a story, a poem, about Jesuits. Our socialists are conscious Jesuits and liars who do not admit that their idol consists of violence to man's conscience and the leveling of mankind to a herd of cattle. My socialist—it's Ivan Karamazov—my socialist is a sincere person who comes right out and admits that he agrees with the Grand Inquisitor's view of humanity and that Christ's faith elevated man to a much higher level than he actually stands. The question is stated in its boldest form: 'Do you despise humanity or admire it, its future saviors?'"

"They all claim that Christ's law is burdensome and abstract, and too heavy for weak people to bear. Instead of the Law of Freedom and Enlightenment, they offer the law of chains and enslavement through bread."

Fyodor agreed. "That's right. But it is clear to me—clearer than ever now—that I cannot answer that position straightforwardly. There is no Euclidian answer to that question. I have to answer it practically and indirectly. So, after Ivan presents his case against God, or God's world, in the next book, the elder Zosima's death and deathbed conversations with his friends occur. He is a saint. I took the character and figure from ancient Russian monks and saints, along with profound humility, boundless, naïve hopes about the future of Russia. He embodies all of Russia's moral and even political mission. Didn't Saint Sergius and the metropolitan Pyotr and Aleksey always have Russia in mind in this sense?"

Solovyev nodded.

"The chapter is exalted and poetic. The prototype is especially Tikhon, Tikhon the monk. And I thought of Father Ambrose too—thank you for taking me to Optina! If I succeed, I will force people to recognize that a pure, ideal Christian is the furthest thing from an abstraction. He is graphically real, possible, standing before our eyes. Christianity, I'll show, is the only refuge of the Russian land from its evils. I pray to God I'll succeed. The whole novel is being written for its sake, but only let it succeed. So much depends on it. Only let this span the land and sea."[9]

"Russia needs to read this."

"I believe so. The fundamental thought is that if you distort the truth of Christ by identifying it with the aims of this world, you instantly lose the meaning of Christianity. Your reason must undoubtedly fall prey to disbelief. Instead of the true ideal of Christ, a new Tower of Babel is constructed."[10]

"A tower of Babel, or a total collapse of everything, beginning with the Palace."

Early in 1880, a bomb had exploded in the basement of the winter palace. Ten soldiers died, though Tsar Alexander and his dinner guests escaped injury. A Populist terrorist group known as People's Will claimed responsibility. They were just getting started. Alexander appointed Count Mikhail Loris-Melikov dictator and gave him authority to quell the terrorist threat; but shortly afterward, a Jewish radical, Ippolit Mlodetsky, shot at Loris-Melikov but missed. Dostoevsky was in the crowd when Mlodetzky was hung in early 1880 in Semenovsky Square, where Dostoevsky had once awaited his own execution. Other assassination attempts followed. Terror was met with vigorous repression, and Russia teetered on the brink of chaos.

"Christ can save us. Christ alone."

"I will drink to that."

≈

"Every new installment of *Karamazov* was sold out, devoured as soon as it appeared. It was as if all of Russia were reading the novel, as if they were looking for some answer to the great Russian problem, as if the novel would guide them through the gloom that seemed to be gathering. I was not just writing a novel. I was engaged in the great debate about the future of Russia. And I was debating on all sides. I spoke in the loudest voice I knew, and it was heard from one end of the land to the other, across the sea."

Maikov struggled to stay awake. He glanced surreptitiously at his pocket watch and saw that it was four in the morning.

"There are the liberals, Westernizers, who want to bring an alien plan to Russia. It will never work. There was no connection to the people of Russia, none at all. And there are the Slavophiles, who love the people but fail to see what Russia really is. They love an imaginary Russia, a Russia without Peter the Great, not the Russia that is the universal people. And there are the socialists who love neither the people nor the West but simply love to tear down everything, beginning with Christ. *Karamazov* stands for Russia, for Christ, for Russia's universal mission in the world. And that is the way forward, the only way forward. It is either that or bombs, assassinations, chaos, terror."

"Christ or nothing," Maikov said through a stifled yawn.

"Christ, or Russia will be reduced to nothing."

13

THE PROPHET

I can sleep on the train," Fyodor protested.

Anna frowned. "You'll miss your stop."

"Maikov, Maikov will wake me up." Maikov bowed slightly in Anna's direction. He was about to fall asleep on his feet.

"If he is awake himself. How much did you drink?"

Fyodor shrugged and spread his hands helplessly and ran his fingers through his thinning hair. "She is a Russian wife, don't you see?"

"And he a Russian husband—a Russian child."

He bowed to Anna's mother and kissed her hand. The children gathered to the door, and Fyodor hugged and kissed each one. Lyubov he held for a long time. He solemnly shook Fedya's hand and then embraced him and sent him off with a tossle of his hair. Then he straightened and pulled Anna close.

"I wish you and the children could go."

"We cannot afford it."

"I promise I will write, every day. Those were her instructions," he added to Maikov. "I will return triumphant, like a Caesar. I will conquer Moscow and bring you the spoils."

Anna held him close and rested her head against his chest. "I will be content if you return."

"I want a lot more than that. I have prepared my speech about Pushkin, and in the most extreme spirit of my convictions. I expect a certain amount of abuse, but I'm not afraid. I should serve my cause, and I will speak without fear."

"Turgenev will be there."

Fyodor winced. "It has been worse than ever with him. Ever since last year, when I confronted him after that speech in Petersburg. 'Tell me!' I cried. 'What is your ideal?! Speak!' He had nothing to say."

"They almost had to pull him away," Anna said with a scold in her voice.

"No matter. Not even Turgenev can spoil my triumph. I will prevail because the truth is with me. Of that I am certain."

Fyodor and Anna kissed and held each other for a long time. Maikov picked up the cases and loaded them into the carriage. He turned and looked at the couple. *What an extraordinary pair they make! What an odd, touching love they have.*

Fyodor walked to the carriage. Once seated, he leaned out and waved at Anna and the children one last time.

"I will be back in a week," he shouted as the carriage clattered away, holding up his index finger.

≈

The Pushkin festival in Moscow in the spring of 1880 gathered writers, artists, and intellectuals from all over Russia to pay respects to Russia's national poet. A great statue of Pushkin, funded by private subscription, was to be unveiled, and the unveiling ceremony was to be surrounded by speeches and dinners and festivals and parties. The Moscow Duma paid all the expenses of the participants. The political import of the event was as important as the literary and artistic significance. Never before had Russians been given so much freedom to express themselves openly, and with the crown's approval. In Petersburg, Dostoevsky had found that, even at the most innocent literary reading, every line, even one written twenty years before, had to be submitted to censors for advance permission. He was astonished that in Moscow the authorities would allow anyone to read something newly written without advance censorship.[1]

The politicking had begun before Dostoevsky arrived. Turgenev and Katkov had long been enemies, and Turgenev had appealed to the organizing committee to prohibit Katkov from speaking. Some even tried to blacklist Dostoevsky himself because of his outburst against Turgenev the previous year, but Dostoevsky had become too powerful to be refused. Turgenev was dispatched to convince Tolstoy to attend, and Turgenev returned shaken and offended, by what he would not say. Rumors spread through the festival participants that Tolstoy had quite lost his mind.[2]

Three days after his arrival, on May 25, Dostoevsky was invited to a dinner in his honor at the Hermitage. Four university professors attended, as did Nikolay Rubinshtein, the director of the Moscow Conservatory who had been put in charge of the music for the festival. Fyodor was astonished at the meal—quail, amazing asparagus, ice cream, a river of fine wines and champagnes, coffee and liqueur after dinner, along with magnificent and expensive cigars.[3] Six speakers rose to celebrate Dostoevsky's "great significance as an artist of worldwide sensitivity," his role as a journalist, and his greatness as a Russian. At the end, Dostoevsky himself rose and gave a speech on Pushkin that produced a great effect.[4]

"I must leave by the twenty-seventh," he announced during the dinner. "I promised Anna that I would stay only a week."

An absolute din arose, cries of "We won't let you go!"

Prince Dolgoruky rose and then turned to Fyodor: "All of Moscow will be grieved and indignant if you leave."

"But I must continue my work on *Karamazov*. I cannot leave it aside any longer. I have deadlines."

"We will speak to Katkov," the prince said. "We will demand that he change the publication schedule. You absolutely must stay."[5]

Katkov agreed, and by the next afternoon, the committee announced that the unveiling would take place in early June. Fyodor agreed to stay on.

≈

On June 6, the Pushkin monument was unveiled. After a mass at the Stratnoi Monastery, a procession marched to the square where the monument was set up. Four orchestras, several choirs, and groups of schoolchildren led the procession. Delegates wore badges and carried wreaths; some waved flags of red, white, and blue, and others had banners that were emblazoned with the titles of poems by Pushkin.[6]

Then everyone got their first look at the monument. Standing on a high pedestal, head bowed in intense contemplation, Pushkin gazed down at his admirers. It was Pushkin in all his Russian glory—the romantic head of curling hair, thick lips sensually parted as if he were beginning to speak, his right hand tucked into his vest over his heart and his left elegantly behind the back of his long cape.

The people were crazed with happiness. Many wept, shook hands, embraced, kissed complete strangers. To the music of Meyerbeer's "The Prophet," the delegations came forward one by one to lay wreaths at the foot of the monument.[7]

≈

June 7. The day of the opening of the official ceremonies. Speeches and celebrations.

Turgenev began the day with a speech of his own. Everyone felt that the majority had selected Turgenev as the point to which all their stored-up enthusiasm could be directed and given vent. They honored Turgenev as if they were recognizing him as the main representative of Russian literature, even as the most direct and worthy heir to Pushkin. Since he was the most distinguished representative of Westernism at the celebration, it was expected that this literary trend would gain the chief role and victory in the upcoming intellectual tournament.[8]

Why does Russia love Pushkin? Turgenev asked. What does it mean for him to be our national poet? "All educated Russians," he said, "all the best people, representatives of the land, the government, academic, literature, and art have gathered here to pay a tribute of grateful love to Pushkin. Why? Because Pushkin gave us poetry. And poetry makes us human. Only when by the creative strength of its elect a people achieves a full, conscious, unique expression in its art, in its poetry, does it thus declare its definitive right to its own place in history. It receives its spiritual physiognomy and its voice—and it enters the fraternity of other peoples who recognize it."

From the first moments, the speech rankled. Turgenev's voice was weak and high-pitched and became a screeching falsetto when he became excited. He screeched on and on.

Pushkin's reputation has suffered, Turgenev observed, but now again the tide is turning. "Youth is returning to reading and studying Pushkin. We cannot but rejoice in this return to poetry. As it has been said of Shakespeare, that everyone who becomes literate must become his new reader, so we may hope that every descendant who stops here before this statue with love, understanding the significance of that love, will prove in that way that he, like Pushkin, has become more Russian and more educated, and a freer person."

Is Pushkin a universal poet? Turgenev asked. No. But the restoration of poetry holds promise. "Someday perhaps a poet will appear who will fully deserve the title of a national-universal poet, which we cannot make up our mind to give to Pushkin, although we do not dare deprive him of it either."[9]

The response of the crowd was tepid.

He has denigrated Pushkin by refusing him the title of national poet, Dostoevsky thought. *His fine distinctions were lost. He spoke to the head and not to the heart, to the elites and not to the people. And he spoke as an outsider, a Westerner, not a Russian or lover of the Russian people.*

Glumly, Dostoevsky left the festival and walked back to his lodgings. As he lay in bed, fighting to sleep, Fyodor realized that Turgenev's speech had opened an opportunity. *Turgenev has members of a claque. My followers have true enthusiasm. Tomorrow, the eighth, is my most fateful day. In the morning, I read my piece. In the morning, I will have my day of triumph.*[10]

≈

Dostoevsky sat as quietly as a mouse at the back of the stage, scribbling in a notebook.[11] Alexsey Plescheev read a poem "To the Memory of Pushkin." Then it was Dostoevsky's turn to speak. It was like nothing he had ever imagined. His Petersburg successes were nothing in comparison. When he came out, the hall thundered with applause, and it was very long before they allowed him to read. He waved, made gestures, begging to be allowed to read. Nothing helped: rapture, enthusiasm.[12] Finally he began to read, speaking simply, absolutely as if he were conversing with an acquaintance. Simply and distinctly, without the slightest digression or unnecessary embellishment, he told the public that he thought of Pushkin as someone who expressed the strivings, hopes, and wishes of that very public—the one listening to him at that moment, in that hall. It was as if he had brought Pushkin himself into the hall.[13]

He began to read his speech, but he was stopped by thunderous applause on absolutely every page, and sometimes at every sentence. He read loudly, with fire.[14]

"'Pushkin is an extraordinary phenomenon and, perhaps, the unique phenomenon of the Russian spirit,' said Gogol. I will add, 'and a prophetic phenomenon.' Yes, in his appearing there is contained, for all us Russians, something incontestably prophetic. Pushkin arrives exactly at the beginning of our true self-consciousness, which had only just begun to exist a whole century after Peter's reforms, and Pushkin's coming mightily aids us in our dark way by a new guiding light. In this sense, Pushkin is a presage and a prophecy. I speak not as a literary critic. I dwell on Pushkin's creative activity only to elucidate my conception of his prophetic significance to us and the meaning I give to the word 'prophecy.'"

Dostoevsky divided Pushkin's career into three periods. "It is said that in his first period Pushkin imitated European poets, above all, Byron. Without doubt, the poets of Europe had a great influence upon the development of his genius, and they maintained their influence all through his life. Nevertheless, even the very earliest poems of Pushkin were not mere imitations, and in them the extraordinary independence of his genius was expressed. Already, in the character of Aleko, the hero of 'The Gipsies,' is exhibited a powerful, profound, and purely Russian idea, later to be expressed in harmonious perfection in 'Onegin,' where almost the same

Aleko appears, not in a fantastic light, but as tangible, real, and comprehensible.

"Aleko marked Pushkin's discovery of a typical Russian type," Dostoevsky intoned, "the unhappy wanderer in his native land, the Russian sufferer of history, whose appearance in our society, uprooted from among the people, was a historic necessity. The type is true and perfectly rendered; it is an eternal type, long since settled in our Russian land. These homeless Russian wanderers are wandering still, and the time will be long before they disappear. If they in our day no longer go to gypsy camps to seek their universal ideals in the wild life of the gypsies and their consolation away from the confused and pointless life of our Russian intellectuals, in the bosom of nature, they launch into socialism, which did not exist in Aleko's day; they march with a new faith into another field and there work zealously, believing, like Aleko, that they will by their fantastic occupations obtain their aims and happiness, not for themselves alone but for all mankind. For the Russian wanderer can find his own peace only in the happiness of all men; he will not be more cheaply satisfied, at least while it is still a matter of theory."

Shouts of approval erupted from the crowd.

"When did this wanderer first appear among us?" Dostoevsky continued when the cheers quieted. "This man was born just at the beginning of the second century after Peter's great reforms, in an intellectual society, uprooted from among the people. It was Pushkin's genius to recognize and describe him so perfectly. This poem of genius is not an imitation! Here already is whispered the Russian solution of the question, 'the accursed question,' in accordance with the faith and justice of the people. 'Humble yourself, proud man, and first of all break down your pride. Humble yourself, idle man, and first of all labor on your native land'—that is the solution according to the wisdom and justice of the people."

Five minutes into the speech, everyone without exception, all hearts, all thoughts, all souls were in his power, and he was pressing his advantage.

"Aleko could not find universal harmony among the gypsies because he had first to discover the truth in himself. Truth is not outside thee, but in thyself. Find thyself in thyself, subdue thyself to thyself, be master of thyself and thou wilt see the truth. Not in things is this truth, not outside thee or abroad, but first of all in thine own labor upon thyself."

Again applause interrupted. Dostoevsky raised a hand for quiet.

"This solution of the question is strongly foreshadowed in Pushkin's poem. Still more dearly is it expressed in 'Eugene Onegin,' which is not a fantastic but a tangible and realistic poem, in which the real Russian life is embodied with a creative power and a perfection such as had not been before Pushkin and perhaps never after him. At the beginning of the poem, he is still half a coxcomb and a man of the world; he had lived too little to be utterly disappointed in life. But he is already visited and disturbed by the demon lord of hidden weariness. Of course he has heard of national ideals, but he does not believe in them. He only believes in the utter impossibility of any work whatever in his native land, and upon those who believe in this possibility—then, as now, but few—he looks with sorrowful derision. Tatiana is different. She is positive and not negative, a type of positive beauty, the apotheosis of the Russian woman, and the poet destined her to express the idea of his poem in the famous scene of the final meeting of Tatiana with Onegin. One may even say that so beautiful or positive a type of the Russian woman has never been created since in our literature, save perhaps the figure of Liza in Turgenev's *A Nest of Gentlefolk*."

Turgenev was on stage when Dostoevsky spoke this tribute. Surprised but pleased, he blew a kiss toward Dostoevsky as the crowd roared its approval.

Dostoevsky's voice was still strong, but it was growing quiet.

"Because of his way of looking down upon people, Onegin did not even understand Tatiana when he met her for the first time, in a remote place, under the modest guise of a pure, innocent girl, who was at first so shy of him. When the lovers meet much later, Tatiana is still the same Tatiana, though she has grown into the great lady of Petersburg. Tormented by the splendid life she leads, worn by this position as lady of society and wife of a great general, she is still a woman of the people, still at heart the same pure peasant girl that Onegin had first known, the same woman who has seen through to Onegin's soul, seen that he is a 'parody.' When he seeks her love, she refuses.

"Did she refuse because she, 'as a Russian woman' (and not a Southern or a French woman), is incapable of a bold step or has not the power to sacrifice the fascination of honors, riches, position in society, the conventions of virtue? No, a Russian woman is brave. But she 'is to another given; to him she will be faithful unto death.' To whom, to what will she be true? To what obligations will she be faithful? Is it to that old general whom she cannot possibly love, whom she married only because 'with tears and adjurations her mother did beseech her,' and in her wronged and wounded soul was there then only despair and neither hope nor ray of light at all? Yes, she is true to that general, to her husband, to an honest man who loves her, respects her, and is proud of her. She married him out of despair. But now he is her husband, and her perfidy will cover him with disgrace and shame and will kill him. Can anyone build his happiness on the unhappiness of another?

"Take Ivan Karamazov's challenge," Fyodor said. "Imagine that you yourself are building a palace of human destiny for the final end of making all men happy and of giving them peace and rest at last. And imagine also that, for that purpose, it is necessary and inevitable to torture to death one single human being, and him not a great soul but even in someone's eyes a ridiculous being, not a Shakespeare but simply an honest old man, the husband of a young wife in whom he believes blindly and whom, although he does not know her heart at all, he respects, of whom he is proud, with whom he is happy and at rest. Could Tatiana's great soul, which had so deeply suffered, have chosen otherwise? No, a pure, Russian soul decides thus: Let me, let me alone be deprived of unhappiness. Let my happiness be infinitely greater than the unhappiness of this old man, and, finally, let no one, not this old man, know and appreciate my sacrifice. But I will not be happy through having ruined another. No, Tatiana could not follow Onegin.

"What Pushkin has done in this story," Dostoevsky insisted, "is define the inmost essence of the high society that stands above the Russian people. He defined the type of the Russian wanderer. Onegin is that wanderer; Tatiana is Russian in her moral beauty and fixity, and she must turn from him because he does not love her but only her outward show of elegance. That is what makes Pushkin the great poet of the people. No single Russian writer, before or after him, did ever associate himself so intimately and fraternally with his people as Pushkin. In Pushkin there is something allied indeed to the people, which in him rises on occasion to some of the most naïve emotions. If Pushkin had not existed, there would not have been expressed with the irresistible force with which it appeared after him (not in all writers, but in a chosen few), our belief in our Russian individuality, our now conscious faith in the people's powers, and finally the belief in our future individual destiny among the family of European nations.

"In the last period, Pushkin becomes a universal poet and embodies in his own poetry the universal scope of Russia's mission. The poet reveals something almost miraculous, never seen or heard at any time or in any nation before. There had been in the literatures of Europe men of colossal artistic genius—a Shakespeare, a Cervantes, a Schiller. But show me one of these great geniuses who possessed such a capacity for universal sympathy as our Pushkin. This capacity, the preeminent capacity of our nation, he shares with our nation, and by that, above all, he is our national poet. Even Shakespeare's Italians, for instance, are almost always Englishmen. Pushkin alone of all world poets possessed the capacity of fully identifying himself with another nationality.

"In this, Pushkin not only prophesies Russia's future but becomes a foretaste of that future, a sign of what Russia is destined to become. I will say deliberately, there had never been a poet with a universal sympathy like Pushkin's. And it is not his sympathy alone but his amazing profundity, the reincarnation of his spirit in the spirit of foreign nations, a reincarnation almost perfect and therefore also miraculous because the phenomenon has never been repeated in any poet in all the world. It is only in Pushkin; and by this, I repeat, he is a phenomenon never seen and never heard of before and, in my opinion, a prophetic phenomenon because . . . because herein was expressed the national spirit of his poetry, the national spirit in its future development, the national spirit of our future, which is already implicit in the present, and it was expressed prophetically. For what is the power of the spirit of Russian nationality if it is not its aspiration after the final goal of universality and omnihumanity? In this he was a seer, in this a prophet.

"This is the significance of Russia's contact with the West that began with Peter the Great. Peter started out his reforms for utilitarian reasons. He wanted to make Russia more efficient and modern, but in course of time, as his idea developed, Peter undoubtedly obeyed some hidden instinct which drew him and his work to future purposes, undoubtedly more vast than narrow utilitarianism. Not in a spirit of enmity (as one might have thought it would have been) but in friendliness and perfect love, we received into our soul the geniuses of foreign nations, all alike without preference of race, able by instinct from almost the very first step to discern, to discount distinctions, to excuse and reconcile them, and therein we already showed our readiness and inclination, which had only just become manifest to ourselves, for a common and universal union with all the races of the great Aryan family. Yes, beyond all doubt, the destiny of a Russian is pan-European and universal. To become a true Russian, to become a Russian fully (in the end of all, I repeat), means only to become the brother of all men, to become, if you will, a universal man.

"Russia's divisions are all wrong-headed. Slavophiles debate Westerners, and Westerners despise Slavophiles. Both fail to see Russia's destiny. To a true Russian, Europe and the destiny of all the mighty Aryan family are as dear as Russia herself, as the destiny of his own native country because our destiny is universality, won not by the sword but by the strength of brotherhood and our fraternal aspiration to reunite mankind.

"This is the Christian destiny of Russia, of the Russia in whose soul Christ still lives. In the course of time I believe that we—not we, of course, but our children to come—will all without exception understand that to be a true Russian does indeed mean to aspire finally to reconcile the contradictions of Europe, to show the end of European yearning in our Russian soul, omni-human and all-uniting. It means to include within our soul by brotherly love all our brethren and at last, it may be, to pronounce the final Word of the great general harmony, the final brotherly communion of all nations in accordance with the law of the gospel of Christ! I know, I know too well, that my words may appear ecstatic, exaggerated, and fantastic. Let them be so; I do not repent having uttered them. They ought to be uttered, above all now, at the moment that we honor our great genius who by his artistic power embodied this idea."

Dostoevsky's final words were pronounced in a sort of inspired whisper, like the incantation of a magus or a prophet. "Do I speak of economic glory, of the glory of the sword or of science? I speak only of the brotherhood of man. I say, to this universal, omni-human union, that the heart of Russia, perhaps more than all other nations, is chiefly predestined. I see its traces in our history, our men of genius, in the artistic genius of Pushkin. Let our country be poor, but this poor land 'Christ traversed with blessing, in the garb of a serf.' Why then should we not contain His final word? Was not He Himself born in a manger? I say again, we at least can already point to Pushkin, to the universality and omni-humanity of his genius. He surely could contain the genius of foreign lands in his soul as his own. In art at least, in artistic creation, he undeniably revealed this universality of the aspiration of the Russian spirit, and therein is a great promise. If our thought is a dream, then in Pushkin at least this dream has solid foundation. Had he lived longer, he would perhaps have revealed great and immortal embodiments of the Russian soul, which would then have been intelligible to our European brethren. He would have attracted them much more and closer than they are attracted now; perhaps he would have succeeded in explaining to them all the truth of our aspirations, and they would understand us more than they do now; they would have begun to have insight into us and would have ceased to look at us so suspiciously and presumptuously as they still do. Had Pushkin lived longer, then among us too there would perhaps be fewer misunderstandings and quarrels than we see now. But God saw otherwise. Pushkin died in the full maturity of his powers and undeniably bore away with him a great secret into the grave. And now we, without him, are seeking to divine his secret."

Fyodor lowered his head and in a deathly silence began rather hurriedly to leave the podium. The hall held its breath, one minute, then another.

From the back rows rang out a hysterical shriek, "You have solved it!" The cry was taken up by several feminine voices in chorus. The entire auditorium began to stir. From every side came the shrieks, "You have solved it. You solved it!" A storm of applause, some sort of rumbling, stamping, feminine screeches. The hall resounded with an unprecedented tempest of ecstasy.[15] Strangers wept, sobbed, embraced each other, and swore to one another to do better, not to hate one another, but instead to love one another. Everyone rushed the platform to see Dostoevsky, to touch him. Highborn ladies, female students, state secretaries, students hugged and kissed him. All the members of the Society who were on the platform hugged and kissed him. They literally wept from delight. Calls went on for half an hour. People waved handkerchiefs. Two men came to Dostoevsky, strangers, and said, "We had been enemies to one another for twenty years, but now we have embraced and been reconciled. It is you who reconciled us, you, our saint, you, our prophet!"

Turgenev rushed up to embrace Dostoevsky. He was crying. The master of ceremonies rushed to the podium to declare that the speech was an historical event, like the sun coming out from behind dark clouds, dissipating everything, illuminating everything. Brotherhood had arrived.

Dostoevsky rushed to the wings to escape, but a crowd of women stopped him. They kissed his hands. Students rushed in, tears streaming down their cheeks, and fell on the floor before him in convulsions.

People stamped and shouted, "Prophet, prophet!"[16]

It took an hour to restore order. Urged to speak by Dostoevsky and others, the Russian critic Aksakov proclaimed that the divisions between Westernizers and Slavophiles had evaporated and a new era of harmony had begun.

Dostoevsky was exhausted. He grew weak and asked to leave. Before he left, a group came on stage with a large laurel wreath and crowned him with it. The Duma thanked him on behalf of the city. Finally he escaped and went to rest for a few hours before he had to perform "The Prophet." That night, he stood and recited.

> With fainting soul athirst for Grace,
> I wandered in a desert place,
> And at the crossing of the ways
> I saw a sixfold Seraph blaze;

> He touched mine eyes with fingers light
> As sleep that cometh in the night:
> And like a frightened eagle's eyes,
> They opened wide with prophecies.

Reciting the poem was another triumph. He recited it twice, each time with such intense passion that his listeners felt uncanny tingling in their hearts and up their spines. His right hand, tremblingly pointing out guilt, clearly refrained from any overwrought gestures. The voice was strained to an outcry.[17]

≈

When he returned to his room, Fyodor could not sleep. Slipping out unnoticed, he went to the Pushkin monument once more. The night was warm, but there was almost no one in the street. Arriving in Strastnaya Square, he lifted with difficulty the enormous laurel wreath that had been presented to him at the morning session after his speech, laid it at the foot of the monument to his great teacher, bowed to the ground before it, and kissed the earth.[18]

> With fainting soul athirst for Grace,
> I wandered in a desert place,
> And at the crossing of the ways
> I saw a sixfold Seraph blaze;
> He touched mine eyes with fingers light
> As sleep that cometh in the night:
> And like a frightened eagle's eyes,

They opened wide with prophecies.
He touched mine ears, and they were drowned
With tumult and a roaring sound:
I heard convulsion in the sky,
And flight of angel hosts on high,
And beasts that move beneath the sea,
And the sap creeping in the tree.
And bending to my mouth he wrung
From out of it my sinful tongue,
And all its lies and idle rust,
And 'twixt my lips a-perishing
A subtle serpent's forkèd sting
With right hand wet with blood he thrust.
And with his sword my breast he cleft,
My quaking heart thereout he reft,
And in the yawning of my breast
A coal of living fire he pressed.
Then in the desert I lay dead,
And God called unto me and said:
"Arise, and let My voice be heard,
Charged with My will go forth and span
The land and sea, and let My word
Lay waste with fire the heart of man."

EPILOGUE

Anna woke to find Fyodor staring at her.

"Light a candle, Anna, and hand me the New Testament. I have been lying here awake for three hours now, and only now I have clearly realized that I shall die today."[1]

She brought him the Testament he had received from Natalya Fonvizina in Siberia. He opened it and read the first passage that appeared to his eye. It was Matthew 13:14–15: "And Jesus said to John, Delay not, for thus it becomes us to fulfill the great truth."

"Do you hear, Anna? Delay not! That means I must die."

Three days before, on January 25, 1881, Fyodor had quarreled with his sister Vera over dinner, left the table in anger, and sat down at the writing table in his Petersburg apartment. As he passed his hand over his face, he realized it was covered with blood from his nose. The following day, he had confessed and taken communion, and then improved slightly. He awoke on January 28 certain that it was the end.

"Call Maikov. No one else. Just Maikov."

Fyodor comforted Anna with tender words and entrusted the children to her care. Before he fell asleep, he said,

"Remember, Anna, I have also loved you passionately and never betrayed you once, not even in thought."[2]

He was awake through the afternoon, Maikov at his bed-side. Lyubov and Fedya came for a final blessing. "Always love and obey your mother," he instructed. He promised Fedya his New Testament and asked that the parable of the prodigal son be read to the children. Near dinnertime, he fell into a coma and never reawakened. Anna held his hand and felt his pulse get feebler and feebler. By the time the doctor arrived, Fyodor was already dead.

Anna was hysterical. "O, whom have I lost! Whom have I lost!"

Involuntarily Maikov broke out, "Whom has Russia lost! Whom has Russia lost!"[3]

ACKNOWLEDGMENTS

All are responsible for all and for everything, Dostoevsky said. While I wrote this book, and my name appears on the cover, I know that I could not have written it without assistance from many others. Aaron Rench first convinced me to contribute to the Christian Encounters Series. I taught Dostoevsky for many years at New St. Andrews College, and I am grateful for the insights I have gathered over the years from students. My father, Dr. Paul Leithart, encouraged me with his usual enthusiastic interest, and conversations with my sons Christian and Woelke helped me clarify how to construct the book. I relied a great deal on real Dostoevsky scholars, who contributed indirectly with their research and insights, none more than Joseph Frank, whose biography is an astonishing achievement in every respect. The editorial staff at Nelson was, once again, superb. They, and many others, are all responsible.

Since the fall of 2010, the face of my granddaughter, Vivian Joyce Leithart, has tiled the background of my office computer. I cannot help but smile whenever I look at her dimpled right cheek, her double chin, her dark eyes. I dedicate this book to her, confident that she belongs to *the* Prophet whose Spirit possessed Dostoevsky, confident, too, that His sixfold Seraph has pressed a coal of fire into her breast and has opened her eyes with wonder, her ears to the roar of the world, her mouth with words of fire.

NOTES

CHAPTER 1

1. Alexander Pushkin, "The Prophet," translated by Maurice Baring in *Maurice Baring Restored: Selections from His Work* (Portsmouth, NH: Heinemann, 1970), 328, available at http://www.artofeurope. com/pushkin/pus1.htm.

2. "monotonous . . ." from Andrey Dostoevsky, quoted in Joseph Frank, *Dostoevsky: A Writer in His Time* (Princeton: Princeton University Press, 2010), 14; "joyless" quoted in Frank, *Dostoevsky*; Dr. Dostoevsky's irritability, rages, and passions from Andrey's description of Dr. Dostoevsky's preparation of Mikhail and Fyodor for a Latin entrance exam, quoted in Frank, *Dostoevsky*, 10, 17.

3. "ecstatic excitement," from Andrey, quoted in Frank, *Dostoevsky*, 15.

4. "natural gaiety" is Marya's own self-description, quoted in Frank, *Dostoevsky*, 9.

5. "good-bye my soul" and "my sweetheart," from letters between Dr. Mikhail and Marya Dostoevsky, quoted in Frank, *Dostoevsky*, 12.

6. "knew Christ and the Gospels," from Dostoevsky quoted in Alexander Boyce Gibson, *The Religion of Dostoevsky* (Louisville: Westminster Press, 1974), 8.

7. "one of the first books that ever made an impression," from Dostoevsky to Anna, quoted in Frank, *Dostoevsky*, 30; "received the seed of God into his heart," Fr. Zosima in *Brothers Karamozov* (trans. Richard Pevear and Larissa Volokhonsky; New York: Farrar, Straus and Giroux, 2002), describing the effect of the book of Job on him as a boy.

8. "I loved nothing in life like the woods with its mushrooms and

wild berries. . . that raw smell of decayed leaves I loved so much," from Dostoevsky, *A Writer's Diary, 1873–1876* (trans. Gary Saul Morson; Evanston: Northwestern University Press, 1997), 353.

9. Description of birch forest from Andrey's memoirs in David Magarshack, *Dostoevsky* (Santa Barbara, CA: Greenwood Press, 1975), 29; "thick, verdant . . . terror" from Fyodor Dostoevsky, quoted in Frank, *Dostoevsky*, 16.

10. "watched the long rows . . . straight furrows," quoted with slight modification from his story, "The Little Hero" in Dostoevsky, *Poor People and a Little Hero* (trans. David Magarshack; New York: Anchor Books, 1968), 214.

11. Description of walking near the wood from Fyodor Dostoevsky, quoted in Frank, *Dostoevsky*, 16.

12. The following page and a half are taken with very minor modifications from Dostoevsky's account of the incident in *Writer's Diary*, 351–354.

13. "like a desert . . . here and there," from Andrey's memoirs, quoted in Frank, *Dostoevsky*, 17.

14. "he also went to visit the huts of the peasants . . . tea," quoted with some modifications from Anna Dostoevsky, *Reminiscences* (trans. Beatrice Stillman; New York: Liveright Publishing, 1977), 296.

15. "tiny and unimportant spot," from Fyodor Dostoevsky, quoted in Frank, *Dostoevsky*, 16.

CHAPTER 2

1. "bitterest time" and "Father was totally destroyed," from Andrey's memoirs, quoted in Frank, *Dostoevsky*, 18.

2. "it was a moving scene . . ." from Andrey's memoirs, quoted in Frank, *Dostoevsky*, 19.

3. "I felt sorry for our poor father," letter from Fyodor to Mikhail, slightly modified to fit the context here; quoted in Frank, *Dostoevsky*, 19.

4. "not a drop of water . . ." from letter of Dr. Dostoevsky to Fyodor, 1839, quoted in Frank, *Dostoevsky*, 47.

5. "tears of my poor father . . ." from letter of Fyodor, quoted in Frank, *Dostoevsky*, 46.

6. "gloomy, ill-humored . . . just his character," modified from *Poor Folk*, applied (speculatively) to Dostoevsky's feelings about his own father in Frank, *Dostoevsky*, 20.

7. "peacock . . . many years," taken with modifications from *Writer's Diary*, 327–328.

8. "Belinsky was the most intense person I have ever met," from *Writer's Diary*, 126; Belinsky "was always, throughout his life, a wholehearted enthusiast," from *Writer's Diary*, 128.

9. These are the words of Belinsky concerning *Poor Folk*, though not in fact quoted to Nekrasov; quoted in Frank, *Dostoevsky*, 76.

10. The descriptions in this paragraph are taken from Dostoevsky's contemporaries at the Military Academy, quoted by William Leatherbarrow, *Fyodor Dostoevsky* (Boston: Twayne Publishers, 1981), 15.

11. "we will carry . . . trumpet his name," the description of the initial reception of Dostoevsky among the Belinsky circle, from Panaev, quoted in Frank, *Dostoevsky*, 86.

12. "a simple novel . . . types," from Belinsky's published review of *Poor Folk*, slightly modified. To our knowledge, these words were not actually spoken to Dostoevsky. Quoted in Frank, *Dostoevsky*, 76.

13. "Gogol makes . . ." paraphrased from Frank, *Dostoevsky*, 299. Frank is summarizing the assessment of Gogol by the character Makar in *Poor Folk*.

14. "suddenly a strange thought . . . councilors," from an essay by Dostoevsky; not spoken to Belinsky; quoted in Leatherbarrow, *Dostoevsky*, 18.

15. This was the scene that Belinsky especially noted; quoted in Frank, *Dostoevsky*, 80.

16. "stopped . . . all my life," from Dostoevsky's own account of his reaction to his meeting with Belinsky, quoted in Frank, *Dostoevsky*, 94; "drunk with glory," from letter of Fyodor to Mikhail, quoted in Frank, *Dostoevsky*, 86–87.

17. "he has fallen in love . . . myself," quoted in Frank, *Dostoevsky*, 87.

18. "terribly nervous . . . talent," description from Mme. Panaev, hostess of the Belinsky circle and Nekrasov's mistress, quoted in Frank, *Dostoevsky*, 88.

19. "ardently attracted . . . never to be repeated in the future," taken with modifications from *Writer's Diary*, 127–128.

CHAPTER 3

1. "scrape . . . fingernail" and "it was covered . . . thick clouds," from reminiscence of D. D. Akshamurov, one of the prisoners; quoted in Frank, *Dostoevsky*, 175.

2. "had always stood out . . . good health," from Akshamurov, quoted in Frank, *Dostoevsky*, 176.

3. "prisoners . . . executed" from Frank, *Dostoevsky*, 177.

4. Quoted in Frank, *Dostoevsky*, 179.

5. For the sake of simplicity and narrative economy, I have conflated several separate meetings. Petrashevsky's attack on the radicalism of Speshnev and his brief in favor of gradual reform, starting with the judicial system, occurred at the April 1, 1849, meeting of the group, while Dostoevsky's reading of the letter from Belinsky occurred two weeks later.

6. "I do not adhere . . . France," quoted in Frank, *Dostoevsky*, 143.

7. "it was an interesting kaleidoscope . . . modest supper," quoted with modifications from Akshamurov; quoted in Frank, *Dostoevsky*, 139.

8. "my Mephistopheles," from Dostoevsky, quoted in Frank, *Dostoevsky*, 152.

9. Quoted in Frank, *Dostoevsky*, 158.

10. "hysterics," from Antonelli's description of the reaction to Belinsky's letters, quoted in Frank, *Dostoevsky*, 157.

11. "stood on the scaffold . . . forgiven much," from *Writer's Diary*, 289.

12. "ten dreadful, infinitely terrible minutes," from *Writer's Diary*, 289.

13. "the ex-officer Dostoevsky knew immediately that his life had been spared," Frank, *Dostoevsky*, 179.

14. "the horses and sledge . . . to tears," from Dostoevsky's letter to Mikhail, quoted in Frank, *Dostoevsky*, 185.

15. Most of this paragraph is taken with modifications from reminiscence of Jaztrzembski, quoted in Frank, *Dostoevsky*, 186.

Chapter 4

1. "coarse . . . pigs," taken with slight modifications from a letter to Mikhail, quoted in Frank, *Dostoevsky*, 188–189.

2. "gave up everything . . . sublime sufferers," taken with modification from a letter of Dostoevsky, quoted in Frank, *Dostoevsky*, 187; and *Writer's Diary*, 130.

3. "courtyard . . . dead," taken, with some modifications, from *The House of the Dead* (trans. Constance Garnett; New York: Barnes and Noble, 2004), 12.

4. "fearless . . . departure of the major," taken, with some modifications, from *House of the Dead*, 12.

5. "he passed . . . breaking up," taken with some modifications from *House of the Dead*, 52.

6. "famous robber . . . seemed natural," taken with some modifications from *House of the Dead*, 58.

7. "The major was . . . departure of the major," taken with some modifications from *House of the Dead*, 18. The scene and conversation that occupies the next few paragraphs is partly fictional, though the sentiments and many of the words are Dostoevsky's own.

8. This statement is taken with modifications from *House of the Dead*, 191.

9. This whole scene is described in *House of the Dead*, 52–53.

10. "They are not fond . . . fond of you," taken with some modification from *House of the Dead*, 34.

11. "It was Easter Sunday . . . after all," from "The Peasant Marey," *Writer's Diary*, 351ff.

12. "morbidly, insanely . . . coined liberty," taken with modifications from *House of the Dead*, 22. The conversation is fictitious, but the sentiments and words are Dostoevsky's.

13. "Have you seen . . . filled with something," from *Writer's Diary*, 142.

14. "sacred feeling . . . fatherland," from an article by Maikov in *St. Petersburg Gazette*, quoted in Frank, *Dostoevsky*, 243.

15. "crimes cannot be compared . . . penal servitude," taken with slight modifications from *House of the Dead*, 53.

16. "the Russian people know the Gospel . . . unconsciously," taken with modifications from *Writer's Diary*, 164.

17. "Do not judge . . ." *Writer's Diary*, 348.

CHAPTER 5

1. "I have never considered . . . all that in you," taken with modifications from a letter of Fyodor to Marya, quoted in Frank, *Dostoevsky*, 231–232. The words are Dostoevsky's, though they were not uttered in this setting.

2. "tear Dostoevsky apart," modified from Wrangel, quoted in Frank, *Dostoevsky*, 233.

3. This description is taken from a letter to Fyodor from Marya, quoted in Frank, *Dostoevsky*, 234.

4. "struck . . . night," from a letter of Dostoevsky describing his reaction to Marya's letter, quoted in Frank, *Dostoevsky*, 234; "dreams . . . torrents," from a letter of Dostoevsky describing his reaction to Marya's affair with Nikolay, quoted in Frank, *Dostoevsky*, 234.

CHAPTER 6

1. Description of Marya's temperament and personality, from Dostoevsky, quoted in Frank, *Dostoevsky*, 241.

2. "serious . . . month," from Suslova's description of Dostoevsky, quoted in Frank, *Dostoevsky*, 387.

3. "round-the-clock . . . mid-afternoon," quoted with modifications from Frank, *Dostoevsky*, 292.

4. The sentiments are expressed in a letter of Dostoevsky to Mikhail, quoted in Frank, *Dostoevsky*, 275.

5. "The Russian idea . . . nationality," from Dostoevsky, quoted in Frank, *Dostoevsky*, 285.

6. "Sacrifice . . . child," quoted from an article by Dostoevsky by Frank, *Dostoevsky*, 297.

7. "pleasant, honest . . . nauseating," taken with some modifications from Dostoevsky, quoted in Frank, *Dostoevsky*, 352.

8. "I remember . . . money from her," from *Winter Notes on Summer Impressions* (trans. David Patterson; Evanston: Northwestern University Press, 1997), 40–41.

9. "it is striking . . . your ideal," from *Winter Notes*, 37.
10. It is not certain that Dostoevsky met the radical revolutionary Bakunin. My inclusion here is more for dramatic purposes than because I am convinced that they did meet.
11. "I often led . . . four," from Strakhov's account of their debate in Italy, quoted in Frank, *Dostoevsky*, 356.
12. The debate between Strakhov and Dostoevsky did include discussion of the mathematical formula, but I am here importing some material from Dostoevsky, *Notes from Underground* (trans. Richard Pevear and Larissa Volokhonsky; New York: Vintage: 1994), Part I.
13. "defect . . . day," from Strakhov's account of their argument in Italy, quoted in Frank, *Dostoevsky*, 356.

CHAPTER 7

1. "At every instant . . . to see this," from Dostoevsky, quoted in Frank, *Dostoevsky*, 403.
2. "It was terrible . . . talkativeness," from Maikov, quoted in Frank, *Dostoevsky*, 403.
3. "divert . . . epilepsy," taken with some modifications from Maikov, quoted in Frank, *Dostoevsky*, 403.
4. "ill . . . because," taken with modification from a letter to Mikhail, written in April 1864, quoted in Frank, *Dostoevsky*, 406.
5. "loved me immeasurably . . . attached to each other," from a letter to Wrangel, quoted in Frank, *Dostoevsky*, 443–444.
6. "she was the most honorable . . . in my life," from a letter to Wrangel, quoted in Frank, *Dostoevsky*, 444.
7. "You are coming too late . . . Good-bye, dear!" directly quoted from a letter of Suslova written in her diary, quoted in Frank, *Dostoevsky*, 390. In reality, Fyodor did not receive the letter until after he had visited Suslova.
8. The entire account is taken from Suslova's diary, which is summarized in Frank, *Dostoevsky*, 390–392. I have compressed a number of weeks, and several different conversations, into a single meeting.
9. Dostoevsky's words here are taken from two letters, one to V. D.

Constant and the other to Mikhail, quoted in Frank,
Dostoevsky, 389.

CHAPTER 8

1. "epoch of dissociation . . . consolation in that," from *Writer's Diary*, 394–395.
2. "Christ alone . . . development," from Dostoevsky's notebook, quoted in Frank, *Dostoevsky*, 407–409.
3. Summary of Dostoevsky's views from his notebooks, summarized in Frank, *Dostoevsky*, 407–409.
4. Quoted in Frank, *Dostoevsky*, 441.
5. "he never tried . . . translator," from *Writer's Diary*, 466–467.
6. "It's necessary . . . too late," taken with modifications from a letter to Wrangel, quoted in Frank, *Dostoevsky*, 440.
7. "two roads . . . choose the first," taken with modifications from a letter to Wrangel, quoted in Frank, *Dostoevsky*, 440.
8. "I owe . . . edit myself," taken with modifications from a letter to Wrangel, quoted in Frank, *Dostoevsky*, 444.
9. Quoted in Frank, *Dostoevsky*, 457.
10. Quoted in Frank, *Dostoevsky*, 456.
11. "situation . . . on time," taken with modifications from a letter to Suslova, quoted in Frank, *Dostoevsky*, 459.
12. "hemmed . . . Shkestakov," taken with modifications from a letter to Suslova, quoted in Frank, *Dostoevsky*, 459.
13. The conversation is fictional but is based on several facts: Dostoevsky did meet Princess Shalikova in Wiesbaden; she was related to Katkov and arranged for Dostoevsky to begin writing for his journal; *The Russian Messenger* was a very conservative journal, and Dostoevsky was regarded as a traitor to reform by publishing his work in it.
14. "It is the psychological report . . . his deed," taken with slight modifications from a letter to Katkov describing the plan for *Crime and Punishment*, quoted in Frank, *Dostoevsky*, 460–461.

CHAPTER 9

1. "the house . . . lived," from Anna's diary, quoted in Frank,

Dostoevsky, 511–512; "dim and hushed . . . cuffs," taken with modifications from Anna's diary, quoted in Frank, *Dostoevsky*, 511–512.

2. "Fyodor . . . street," taken with minor modifications from an account by one of those present when Fyodor made the announcement, quoted in Frank, *Dostoevsky*, 464.

3. "All those high school . . . freedom," taken directly from a letter of Dostoevsky to Katkov, quoted in Frank, *Dostoevsky*, 466–467.

4. "Do you know . . . thought," taken directly from a letter to Katkov, quoted in Frank, *Dostoevsky*, 467.

5. "how can . . . inexperienced," taken directly from a letter to Katkov, quoted in Frank, *Dostoevsky*, 467.

6. "makes my blood boil," from Anna's diary, quoted in Frank, *Dostoevsky*, 513. The scene here is fiction, but the words I put in Anna's mouth accurately capture her response.

7. "wise, good . . . in her," taken with modifications from Anna's diary, quoted in Frank, *Dostoevsky*, 513.

8. This was an actual conversation, taken with modification from Anna's diary, quoted in Frank, *Dostoevsky*, 515.

9. "will certainly propose . . . illness," taken with modifications from Anna's diary, quoted in Frank, *Dostoevsky*, 515.

Chapter 10

1. "heightened . . . face," description taken from Anna's diary, quoted in Frank, *Dostoevsky*, 518.

2. This conversation is taken with modifications from the account of Fyodor's proposal in Anna Dostoevsky, *Reminiscences*, quoted in Frank, *Dostoevsky*, 518.

3. "felt cold . . . stand still," taken with slight modifications from Anna Dostoevsky, *The Diary of Dostoevsky's Wife* (trans. Madge Pemberton; ed. Rene Fulop-Miller and Fr. Eckstein; New York: Macmillan, 1928), 50.

4. "Fyodor was in the room . . . melancholy," taken from Anna's *Diary*, 52.

5. "gave out . . . topple," quoted from Anna's *Reminiscences*, 79.

6. "love . . . happiness," taken with modifications from Anna's *Reminiscences*, 112.

7. "pawn . . . acquired," from Anna's *Reminiscences*, 109.

8. "butter . . . execrable," from Anna's *Diary*, 153.

9. Quoted in Frank, *Dostoevsky*, 551.

10. "Hussar . . . tongue," taken from Anna's *Diary*, 57.

11. "rifle . . . husband," from Anna's *Diary*, 57–58.

12. "nervy . . . married me," from Anna's *Diary*, 58.

13. "perpetual quarreling . . . melt away," from Anna's *Diary*, 63.

14. "handsome young German . . . suspicions," from Anna's *Diary*, 72.

15. "shivering . . . covering," from Anna's *Diary*, 159.

16. "laughing . . . easy to take in," from Anna's *Diary*, 63.

17. "want to be cross . . . joke," from Anna's *Diary*, 118.

18. "hat suits . . . child," from Anna's *Diary*, 117.

19. "don't kill . . . don't kill," taken from Anna's *Diary*, 120. For Fyodor sticking out his tongue, see Anna's *Diary*, 131.

20. "about us . . . hatchet," from Anna's *Diary*, 135.

21. "horrifies . . . real dead body," taken with some modifications from Anna's *Diary*, 419.

22. "crawl . . . proud of it," taken with significant modifications from Dostoevsky's account of the meeting, quoted in Frank, *Dostoevsky*, 546–547.

23. "a person . . . others," taken from a letter of Turgenev that gave Turgenev's own account of his meeting with Dostoevsky, which contrasted radically with Dostoevsky's account, quoted in Frank, *Dostoevsky*, 548. These words were not actually spoken to Dostoevsky.

24. "read . . . Papa," Anna's *Diary*, 42.

25. "at the present moment . . . legitimate as reality," from *Writer's Diary*, 214–215.

26. "Sonya . . . novel," from a letter to Maikov, quoted in Frank, *Dostoevsky*, 567.

27. "This tiny . . . might live," from Dostoevsky's letter to Maikov, quoted in Frank, *Dostoevsky*, 572.

28. "Anya . . . bound by gambling," quoted in Frank, *Dostoevsky*, 613.

29. "dreadfully touchy . . . husband," from Anna's *Diary*, 156.

CHAPTER 11

1. "They began . . . peace," quoted in Frank, *Dostoevsky*, 555.
2. "The Petersburg police . . . full well," from letter to Maikov, quoted in Frank, *Dostoevsky*, 573.
3. "diverse and multifarious . . . villain," *Writer's Diary*, 286.
4. "A year before . . . interesting," from *Demons* (trans. Richard Pevear and Larissa Volokhonsky; New York: Everyman's Library, 2000), 85.
5. Quoted in Frank, *Dostoevsky*, 679.
6. "madman . . . feeble-minded," taken with some modification from Vsevolod Solovyev, quoted in Frank, *Dostoevsky*, 681.
7. Quoted in Frank, *Dostoevsky*, 683.
8. "At one time . . . all mankind," taken with some modifications from N. S. Rusanov, quoted in Frank, *Dostoevsky*, 684.
9. "in this way . . . social life," taken with modification from Prince Peter Kropotkin, quoted in Frank, *Dostoevsky*, 688–689.
10. "If you were . . . axiom," taken with modifications from *Writer's Diary*, 288.

CHAPTER 12

1. "sat like herrings . . . dreamed about her," modified from letters of Dostoevsky, quoted in Frank, *Dostoevsky*, 695–697.
2. "less dry coughing . . . new novels," modified from letters of Dostoevsky, quoted in Frank, *Dostoevsky*, 696–697.
3. "read Job . . . infant," from a letter of Dostoevsky, quoted in Frank, *Dostoevsky*, 704.
4. "crushed . . . recognize her," Anna's *Reminiscences*, 292.
5. "met . . . three times," Anna's *Reminiscences*, 294.
6. "every time I weep . . . rejoices," taken with slight modifications from *Brothers Karamazov* (trans. Richard Pevear and Larissa Volokhonsky; New York: Farrar, Straus, Giroux, 2002), 50. It is Father Zosima's advice to a mother who has lost a son.
7. "I consider . . . next," taken with slight modifications from Dostoevsky, quoted in Frank, *Dostoevsky*, 797.
8. "no one at present . . . be a Catholic," taken with slight modifications from Solovyev's lectures on Godmanhood, quoted in Frank, *Dostoevsky*, 772.

9. "contemporary negator . . . succeed," these paragraphs taken from Dostoevsky's letter to his editor Lyubimov, explaining the purpose of the Grand Inquisitor story, quoted in Frank, *Dostoevsky*, 791–793.

10. "fundamental thought . . . constructed," Dostoevsky's opening remarks before a reading of the Grand Inquisitor story at the University of St. Petersburg, quoted in Frank, *Dostoevsky*, 802.

Chapter 13

1. "most innocent literary reading . . . advance censorship," taken with slight modifications from a letter of Dostoevsky, quoted in Frank, *Dostoevsky*, 813.

2. "quite lost his mind," quotation from Katkov, quoted in Frank, *Dostoevsky*, 817.

3. "quail . . . cigars," taken with some modifications from a letter of Dostoevsky, quoted in Frank, *Dostoevsky*, 815.

4. "great significance . . . great effect," taken with some modifications from a letter of Dostoevsky, quoted in Frank, *Dostoevsky*, 815.

5. The description here conflates separate events. Prince Dolgoruky did not speak at the dinner, but he did persuade the committee to admonish Dostoevsky to stay. The events are recounted in Frank, *Dostoevsky*, 816.

6. "Four orchestras . . . Pushkin," taken with some modifications from Frank, *Dostoevsky*, 819, who is quoting from Marcus Levitt, *Russian Literary Politics and the Pushkin Celebration of 1880* (New York: Cornell University Press, 1989), 83–85.

7. The description is taken with modifications from Frank, *Dostoevsky*, 819.

8. "Everyone felt . . . tournament," taken with slight modifications from Nikolai Strakhov, quoted in Levitt, *Russian Literary Politics*, 106.

9. My account of Turgenev's speech is drawn from Frank, *Dostoevsky*, 821–823; and Levitt, *Russian Literary Politics*, 106–110.

10. "tomorrow . . . read my piece," taken with modifications from letters of Dostoevsky, quoted in Frank, *Dostoevsky*, 824.

11. "quietly . . . notebook," from a reminiscence of the event by Gleb Uspensky, quoted in Frank, *Dostoevsky*, 825.

12. "like nothing he had ever . . . enthusiasm," from letter of Dostoevsky, quoted in Frank, *Dostoevsky*, 824–825.

13. "speaking simply . . . into the hall," taken with slight modifications from Gleb Uspensky's reminiscence, quoted in Frank, *Dostoevsky*, 825.

14. "stopped . . . fire," from a letter of Dostoevsky to Anna, quoted in Frank, *Dostoevsky*, 825. The translation of the Pushkin speech is by S. Koteliansky and J. Middleton Murray, and published in Dostoevsky, *Pages from the Journal of An Author* (Boston: John Luce, 1916), 47–68, available in full at GoogleBooks.

15. from a description of the event by D. A. Lyuabimov, quoted in Frank, *Dostoevsky*, 830–831.

16. "Strangers wept . . . Prophet, prophet," from Dostoevsky's letter to Anna, quoted in Frank, *Dostoevsky*, 831–832.

17. "recited . . . outcry," from Strakhov's recollections of the event, quoted by Frank, *Dostoevsky*, 832.

18. "he went to the Pushkin . . . before it," from Anna's diary, quoted in Frank, *Dostoevsky*, 833. The kiss of the ground is not factual, though, given the fact that Dostoevsky's characters frequently embrace and kiss the earth, not implausible.

EPILOGUE

1. "Light . . . today," quoted in Anna's *Reminiscences*, 345–346.

2. "Remember . . . thought," quoted in Anna's *Reminiscences*, 346.

3. "Whom have I lost . . . Russia lost," quoted in Frank, *Dostoevsky*, 926. In fact, Boleslav Markevich, another writer, was also present at Fyodor's death.

BIBLIOGRAPHY

Dostoevsky, Anna. *The Diary of Dostoevsky's Wife*. Translated by Madge Pemberton. Edited by Rene Fulop-Miller and Fr. Eckstein. New York: Macmillan, 1928.

Dostoevsky, Anna. *Reminiscences*. Translated by Beatrice Stillman. New York: Liveright Publishing, 1977.

Dostoevsky, Fyodor. *Brothers Karamazov*. Translated by Richard Pevear and Larissa Volokhonsky. New York: Farrar, Straus and Giroux, 2002.

Dostoevsky, Fyodor. *Demons*. Translated by Richard Pevear and Larissa Volokhonsky. New York: Everyman's Library, 2000.

Dostoevsky, Fyodor. *The House of the Dead*. Translated by Constance Garnett. New York: Barnes and Noble, 2004.

Dostoevsky, Fyodor. *Notes from the Underground*. Tranlsated by Richard Pevear and Larissa Volokhonsky. New York: Vintage, 1994.

Dostoevsky, Fyodor. *Pages from the Journal of an Author*. Boston: John Luce, 1916.

Dostoevsky, Fyodor. *Poor Folk*, first published in 1846.

Dostoevsky, Fyodor. *Poor People and a Little Hero*. Translated by David Magarshack. New York: Anchor Books, 1968.

Dostoevsky, Fyodor. *Winter Notes on Summer Impressions*. Translated by David Patterson. Evanston: Northwestern University Press, 1997.

Dostoevsky, Fyodor. *A Writer's Diary, 1873–1876*. Translated by Gary

Saul Morson. Evanston: Northwestern University Press, 1997.

Frank, Joseph. *Dostoevsky: A Writer in His Time*. Princeton: Princeton University Press, 2010.

Gibson, Alexander Boyce. *The Religion of Dostoevsky*. Louisville: Westminster Press, 1974.

Leatherbarrow, William. *Fyodor Dostoevsky*. Boston: Twayne Publishers, 1981.

Levitt, Marcus. *Russian Literary Politics and the Pushkin Celebration of 1880*. New York: Cornell University Press, 1989.

Magarshack, David. *Dostoevsky*. Santa Barbara, CA: Greenwood Press, 1975.

Pushkin, Alexander. "The Prophet." Translated by Maurice Baring in *Maurice Baring Restored: Selections from His Work*. (Portsmouth, NH: Heinemann, 1970), 328. Available at http://www.artofeurope.com/pushkin/pus1.htm.

ABOUT THE AUTHOR

D r. Peter Leithart has taught theology and literature at New Saint Andrews College since 1998, and since 2003 has served as pastor of Trinity Reformed Church in Moscow, Idaho.

He received a master of arts in religion and a master of theology from Westminster Theological Seminary in Philadelphia. In 1998, he received his PhD at the University of Cambridge in England. He has authored several books, including *Against Christianity*, *Brightest Heaven of Invention*, *A Son to Me*, and *A House for My Name*. His articles have appeared in the *Atlanta Journal-Constitution*, *Birmingham News*, *Dallas Morning News*, *First Things*, *Modern Theology*, *The International Journal of Systematic Theology*, *The Tyndale Bulletin*, and other publications. He is currently a contributing editor to *Touchstone* magazine. Dr. Leithart and his wife, Noel, have ten children.

Close Encounters of the Christian Kind

— Available Now —

JANE AUSTEN
9781595553027

ANNE BRADSTREET
9781595551098

WILLIAM F. BUCKLEY
9781595550651

JOHN BUNYAN
9781595553041

WINSTON CHURCHILL
9781595553065

ISAAC NEWTON
9781595553034

SAINT FRANCIS
9781595551078

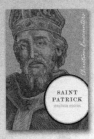

SAINT PATRICK
9781595553058

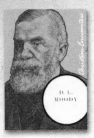

D. L. MOODY
9781595550477

**SAINT NICHO-
LAS**
9781595551153

**SERGEANT
YORK**
9781595550255

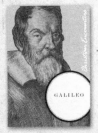

GALILEO
9781595550316

**JOHANN
SEBASTIAN BACH**
9781595551085

**GEORGE
WASHINGTON CARVER**
9781595553034

**J. R. R.
TOLKIEN**
9781595551078